みんなの日本語初級Ⅰ
翻訳・文法解説ローマ字版【英語】

Minna no Nihongo Ⅰ

Translation & Grammatical Notes
Romanized Edition English

スリーエーネットワーク

© 2000 by 3A Corporation

All rights reserved. No part of this publication may be reproduced, stored in a retrieval system, or transmitted in any form or by any means, electronic, mechanical, photocopying, recording, or otherwise, without the prior written permission of the Publisher.

Published by 3A Corporation
Shoei Bldg., 6-3, Sarugaku-cho 2-chome, Chiyoda-ku, Tokyo 101-0064, Japan

ISBN4-88319-165-6 C0081

First published 2000
Printed in Japan

FOREWORD

As the title **Minna no Nihongo** indicates, this book has been designed to make the study of Japanese as enjoyable and interesting as possible for students and teachers alike. Over three years in the planning and compilation, it stands as a complete textbook in itself while acting as a companion volume to the highly regarded **Shin Nihongo no Kiso.**

As readers may know, **Shin Nihongo no Kiso** is a comprehensive introduction to elementary Japanese that serves as a highly efficient resource enabling students wishing to master basic Japanese conversation to do so in the shortest possible time. As such, although it was originally developed for use by AOTS's technical trainees, it is now used by a wide range of people both in Japan and abroad.

The teaching of Japanese is branching out in many different ways. Japanese economic and industrial growth has led to a greater level of interchange between Japan and other countries, and non-Japanese from a wide variety of backgrounds have come to Japan with a range of different objectives and are now living within local communities here. The changes in the social milieu surrounding the teaching of Japanese that have resulted from this influx of people from other countries have in turn influenced the individual situations in which Japanese is taught. There is now a greater diversity of learning needs, and they require individual responses.

It is against this background, and in response to the opinions and hopes expressed by a large number of people who have been involved in the teaching of Japanese for many years both in Japan and elsewhere, that 3A Corporation proudly publishes **Minna no Nihongo.** While the book continues to make use of the clarity and ease of understanding provided by the special features, key learning points and learning methods of **Shin Nihongo no Kiso**, the scenes, situations and characters in **Minna no Nihongo** have been made more universal in order to appeal to a wider range of learners. Its contents have been enhanced in this way to allow all kinds of students to use it for studying Japanese with pleasure.

Minna no Nihongo is aimed at anyone who urgently needs to learn to communicate in Japanese in any situation, whether at work, school, college or in their local community. Although it is an introductory text, efforts have been made to make the exchanges between Japanese and foreign characters in the book reflect Japanese social conditions and everyday life as faithfully as possible. While it is intended principally for those who have already left full-time education, it can also be recommended as an excellent textbook for university entrance courses as well as short-term intensive courses at technical colleges and universities.

We at 3A Corporation are continuing actively to produce new study materials designed to meet the individual needs of an increasingly wide range of learners, and we sincerely hope that readers will continue to give us their valued support.

In conclusion, I should like to mention the extensive help we received in the preparation of this text, in the form of suggestions and comments from various quarters and trials of the materials in actual lessons, for which we are extremely grateful. 3A Corporation intends to continue extending its network of friendship all over the world through activities such as the publishing of Japanese study materials, and we hope that everyone who knows us will continue to lend us their unstinting encouragement and support in this.

Iwao Ogawa
President, 3A Corporation
March 1998

EXPLANATORY NOTES

I. Structure

The learning materials consist of a Main Text, a Translation and Grammar Text and a set of cassette tapes/CDs. The Translation and Grammar Text is currently available in English. Versions in other languages will be published shortly.

The materials have been prepared with the main emphasis on listening and speaking Japanese; they do not provide instruction in reading and writing hiragana, katakana or kanji.

II. Content and Method of Use

1. Main Text

1) Japanese Pronunciation

This section gives examples of the main characteristics of Japanese pronunciation.

2) Classroom instructions, greetings, numerals

These are useful for understanding classroom instructions and daily greetings. They are frequently used by teachers in class.

3) Lessons

There are 25 lessons, and each contains the following:

① Sentence Patterns

Basic sentence patterns are shown in the order they appear.

② Example Sentences

A small dialogue in the style of a question and answer is given to show how the sentence patterns are used in practical conversation. New adverbs, conjunctions, and other grammatical points are also introduced.

③ Conversation

In the conversations, various foreign people staying in Japan appear in a variety of situations. The conversations include everyday expressions and greetings. As they are simple, learning them by heart is recommended. If time allows, students should try developing the conversation by applying the reference words given in each lesson of the Translation and Grammar Text in order to maximize their communication skills.

④ Drills

The drills are divided into three levels: A, B, and C.

Drill A is visually designed in chart style to help understanding of the grammatical structure. The style helps students to learn systematically the basic sentence patterns through substitution drills, and applying verb forms and conjugations following the chart.

Drill B has various drill patterns to strengthen students' grasp of the basic sentence patterns. Follow the directions given in each practice. Drills marked with a ☞ sign use pictorial charts.

Drill C is given in discourse style to show how the sentence patterns function in actual situations, and to enhance practical oral skills. Do not simply read, repeat and substitute, but try making your own substitution, enrich the content, and develop the story.

⑤ Practice

Two kinds of practices are given: one type for listening (👂) and the other for grammar practice.

The listening practice is further divided into a question asking for a personal answer, and a question confirming the key point of the given discourse. The listening practices are designed to strengthen students' aural skills, while the grammar practices check comprehension of vocabulary and the grammar points in the lessons studied.

The reading practices mostly require students to give a true or false response after reading a simple story compiled with words and sentence patterns from the lessons learned.

⑥ Review

This is provided to enable students to go over the essential points every several lessons studied.

⑦ Summary

At the end of the Main Text, a summary of grammatical points is given, such as the use of the particles, verb forms, adverbs and conjunctions, using example sentences appearing in the respective lessons.

⑧ Index

This includes classroom instructions, greetings, numerals, new vocabulary, and idiomatic expressions introduced in each lesson of the Main Text.

2. Translation and Grammar Text

1) **Explanations of the general features and pronunciation of Japanese as well as the Japanese writing system**

2) **Translation of classroom instructions and greetings in the Main Text**

3) **The following are given in each of the 25 lessons.**
   ① new vocabulary and its translation
   ② translation of Sentence Patterns, Example Sentences, and Conversation
   ③ useful words related to the lesson and small pieces of information on Japan and the Japanese
   ④ explanation of essential grammar appearing in the lesson

4) **Translation of the particles, how to use the forms, adverbs and adverbial expressions, and various conjugations found at the back of the Main Text**

5) **Tables showing how to express numbers, time, periods of time, and counters, etc. including items which the textbook does not cover**

3. Cassette Tapes/CDs

On the cassette tapes/CDs, Vocabulary, Sentence Patterns, Example Sentences, Drill C, Conversation and listening comprehension questions of the Practice section are recorded.

Students should pay attention to the pronunciation and intonation when listening to the Vocabulary, Sentence Patterns and Example Sentences. When listening to Drill C and Conversation, try to get accustomed to the natural speed of the language.

4. Romanization

1) In general, the Hepburn system of romanization has been used.
   The syllabic nasal sound is represented by 'n' throughout.

2) Long vowels are indicated as follows:
   ā, ii, ū, ei(ē), ō

e.g., okāsan (mother) ōkii (big, large) tokei (watch, clock) onēsan (elder sister)

3) For readability, the text has been transliterated with spaces between words. Particles are written separately except when accepted as forming a single unit with the parent word.

e.g., nanika (something) desukara (therefore, so)

4) Prefixes, suffixes and counters are usually separated from their parent words by hyphens, and long compound words are broken up by hyphens.

e.g., o-shigoto (work, business) Tanaka-san (Mr. Tanaka)
25-sai (25 years old) hana-ya (flower shop) benkyō-shimasu (study)

However, the hyphen is omitted when the compound is regarded as a single unit.

e.g., hitotsu (one) hitori (one person) ocha (tea) asagohan (breakfast)
oyasuminasai (good night)

5) Capitals are used at the beginning of sentences and for the initial letters of proper nouns.

6) Foreign names are spelt according to the katakana spelling.

e.g., Mirā-san (Mr. Miller)

7) Some foreign loan words are romanized to approximate their original pronunciation.

e.g., pātii (party) fōku (fork)

5. Miscellaneous

1) Words which can be omitted from a sentence are enclosed in square brackets [ ].

e.g., Chichi wa 54 [-sai] desu. (My father is 54 years old.)

2) Synoyms are enclosed in round brackets ( ).

e.g., dare (donata) (who)

3) An alternative word is shown by ～.

e.g., ～ wa ikaga desu ka. (Won't you have ～?/Would you like to have～?)

However a hyphen is used when the alternative words are numbers.

e.g, －sai (－years old) －en (－yen) －jikan (－hours)

TO USERS OF THIS TEXTBOOK
The most effective way to study

1. Learn each word carefully.

The *Translation & Grammatical Notes* introduces the new words for each lesson. First, listen to the tape/CD and learn these words thoroughly, paying special attention to the correct pronunciation and accent. Try to make sentences with the new words. It is important to memorize not only a word itself, but its use in a sentence.

2. Practice the sentence patterns.

Make sure you understand the meaning of each sentence pattern, and do *Drills A* and *B* until you have mastered the pattern. Say the sentences aloud, especially when doing *Drill B*.

3. Practice the conversation drills.

Sentence-pattern practice is followed by conversation practice. The example conversations show the various situations in actual daily life in which people from abroad will often need to use Japanese. Start by doing *Drill C* to get accustomed to the pattern. Don't practice only the dialogue pattern, but try to expand the dialogue. And learn how to communicate suitably according to the situations by practicing the conversation.

4. Listen to the cassette tape/CD repeatedly.

When practicing *Drill C* and *Conversation*, listen to the tape/CD and say the dialogue aloud to make sure you acquire the correct pronunciation and intonation. Listening to the tape/CD is the most effective way to get used to the sound and speed of Japanese and to improve your listening ability.

5. Always remember to review and prepare.

So as not to forget what you have learned in class, always review it the same day. Finally, do the questions at the end of each lesson in order to check what you have learnt and to test your listening comprehension. And, if you have time, look through the words and grammar explanation for the next lesson. Basic preparation is necessary for effective study.

6. Use what you have learnt.

Don't limit your learning to the classroom. Try to talk to Japanese people. Using what you have just learnt is the best way to progress.

If you complete this textbook following the above suggestions, you will have acquired the basic vocabulary and expressions necessary for daily life in Japan.

CHARACTERS IN THE CONVERSATIONS

Mike Miller

American, employee of IMC

Sato Keiko

Japanese, employee of IMC

Jose Santos

Brazilian, employee of Brazil Air

Maria Santos

Brazilian, housewife

Karina

Indonesian, student at Fuji University

Wang Xue

Chinese, doctor at Kobe Hospital

Yamada Ichiro

Japanese, employee of IMC

Yamada Tomoko

Japanese, bank clerk

Matsumoto Tadashi
Japanese,
department chief at IMC

Matsumoto Yoshiko
Japanese, housewife

Kimura Izumi
Japanese, announcer

― Other Characters ―

Watt
British,
professor at Sakura University

Schmidt
German,
engineer at Power Electric Company

Lee
Korean,
research worker at AKC

Teresa
Brazilian, schoolgirl (9 yrs.),
daughter of Jose & Maria Santos

Taro
Japanese, schoolboy (8 yrs.),
son of Ichiro & Tomoko Yamada.

Gupta
Indian, employee of IMC

Thawaphon
Thai, student at Japanese language school

※IMC (computer software company)
※AKC (Ajia-kenkyū-sentā: Asia Research Institute)

CONTENTS

INTRODUCTION ·· 2
   I. General Features of Japanese
   II. Japanese Script
   III. Pronunciation of Japanese

PRELIMINARY LESSON ·· 8
   I. Pronunciation
   II. Classroom Instructions
   III. Daily Greetings and Expressions
   IV. Numerals

TERMS USED FOR INSTRUCTION ·· 10

ABBREVIATIONS ·· 11

LESSON 1 ·· 12
I. Vocabulary	IV. Grammar Explanation
II. Translation	1. N₁ *wa* N₂ *desu*
Sentence Patterns & Example Sentences	2. N₁ *wa* N₂ *ja arimasen*
Conversation:	3. S *ka*
How do you do?	4. N *mo*
III. Reference Words & Information:	5. N₁ *no* N₂
COUNTRY, PEOPLE & LANGUAGE	6. ~*san*

LESSON 2 ·· 18
I. Vocabulary	IV. Grammar Explanation
II. Translation	1. *kore/sore/are*
Sentence Patterns & Example Sentences	2. *kono* N/*sono* N/*ano* N
Conversation:	3. *sō desu/sō ja arimasen*
This is just a token	4. S₁ *ka,* S₂ *ka*
III. Reference Words & Information:	5. N₁ *no* N₂
FAMILY NAMES	6. *Sō desu ka*

LESSON 3 24
I. Vocabulary
II. Translation
Sentence Patterns & Example Sentences
Conversation:
I'll take it
III. Reference Words & Information:
DEPARTMENT STORE

IV. Grammar Explanation
1. *koko/soko/asoko/kochira/sochira/achira*
2. N₁ *wa* N₂ (place) *desu*
3. *doko/dochira*
4. N₁ *no* N₂
5. The *ko/so/a/do* system of demonstrative words
6. *o-kuni*

LESSON 4 30
I. Vocabulary
II. Translation
Sentence Patterns & Example Sentences
Conversation:
What are your opening hours?
III. Reference Words & Information:
PHONE & LETTER

IV. Grammar Explanation
1. *Ima -ji -fun desu*
2. V-*masu*
3. V-*masu*/ V-*masen*/ V-*mashita*/ V-*masendeshita*
4. N (time) *ni* V
5. N₁ *kara* N₂ *made*
6. N₁ *to* N₂
7. S *ne*

LESSON 5 36
I. Vocabulary
II. Translation
Sentence Patterns & Example Sentences
Conversation:
Does this train go to Koshien?
III. Reference Words & Information:
NATIONAL HOLIDAYS

IV. Grammar Explanation
1. N (place) *e ikimasu/kimasu/kaerimasu*
2. *Doko [e] mo ikimasen/ ikimasendeshita*
3. N (vehicle) *de ikimasu/kimasu/kaerimasu*
4. N (person/animal) *to* V
5. *itsu*
6. S *yo*

LESSON 6 ·· 42

I. **Vocabulary**

II. **Translation**
   Sentence Patterns & Example Sentences
   Conversation:
   　Won't you join us?

III. **Reference Words & Information:**
   FOOD

IV. **Grammar Explanation**
   1. N *o* V (transitive)
   2. N *o shimasu*
   3. *Nani o shimasu ka*
   4. *nan* and *nani*
   5. N (place) *de* V
   6. V-*masen ka*
   7. V-*mashō*
   8. *o* ~

LESSON 7 ·· 48

I. **Vocabulary**

II. **Translation**
   Sentence Patterns & Example Sentences
   Conversation:
   　Hello

III. **Reference Words & Information:**
   FAMILY

IV. **Grammar Explanation**
   1. N (tool/means) *de* V
   2. "Word/Sentence" *wa* ~ *go de nan desu ka*
   3. N (person) *ni agemasu*, etc.
   4. N (person) *ni moraimasu*, etc.
   5. *Mō* V-*mashita*

LESSON 8 ·· 54

I. **Vocabulary**

II. **Translation**
   Sentence Patterns & Example Sentences
   Conversation:
   　It's almost time to leave

III. **Reference Words & Information:**
   COLOR & TASTE

IV. **Grammar Explanation**
   1. Adjectives
   2. N *wa na*-adj *[ná]desu*
   　 N *wa i*-adj (~*i*) *desu*
   3. *na*-adj *na* N
   　 i-adj (~*i*) N
   4. *totemo/amari*
   5. N *wa dō desu ka*
   6. N_1 *wa donna* N_2 *desu ka*
   7. S_1 *ga*, S_2
   8. *dore*

LESSON 9 ···60
I. Vocabulary
II. Translation
    Sentence Patterns & Example Sentences
    Conversation:
        That's too bad
III. Reference Words & Information:
    MUSIC, SPORTS & MOVIES

IV. Grammar Explanation
1. N *ga arimasu/wakarimasu*
   N *ga suki desu/kirai desu/ jōzu desu/heta desu*
2. *donna* N
3. *yoku/daitai/takusan/sukoshi/ amari/zenzen*
4. S₁ *kara*, S₂
5. *dōshite*

LESSON 10 ···66
I. Vocabulary
II. Translation
    Sentence Patterns & Example Sentences
    Conversation:
        Do you have chili sauce in this store?
III. Reference Words & Information:
    INSIDE THE HOUSE

IV. Grammar Explanation
1. N *ga arimasu/imasu*
2. N₁ (place) *ni* N₂ *ga arimasu/imasu*
3. N₁ *wa* N₂ (place) *ni arimasu/imasu*
4. N₁ (thing/person/place) *no* N₂ (position)
5. N₁ *ya* N₂
6. Word (s) *desu ka*
7. *Chiri-sōsu wa arimasen ka*

LESSON 11 ···72
I. Vocabulary
II. Translation
    Sentence Patterns & Example Sentences
    Conversation:
        Please send this by sea mail
III. Reference Words & Information:
    MENU

IV. Grammar Explanation
1. Saying numbers
2. Quantifier (period) *ni-kai* V
3. Quantifier *dake*/N *dake*

LESSON 12 ···78
I. Vocabulary
II. Translation
    Sentence Patterns & Example Sentences
    Conversation:
        How was the Festival?
III. Reference Words & Information:
    FESTIVALS & PLACES OF NOTE

IV. Grammar Explanation
1. Past tense of noun sentences and *na*-adjective sentences
2. Past tense of *i*-adjective sentences
3. N₁ *wa* N₂ *yori* adjective *desu*
4. N₁ *to* N₂ *to dochira ga* adjective *desu ka*
   ···N₁/N₂ *no hō ga* adjective *desu*
5. N₁ [*no naka*]*de nani/doko/dare/ itsu ga ichiban* adjective *desu ka*
   ···N₂ *ga ichiban* adjective *desu*

LESSON 13 ··········· 84
I. Vocabulary
II. Translation
   Sentence Patterns & Example Sentences
   Conversation:
      Charge us separately
III. Reference Words & Information:
   TOWN

IV. Grammar Explanation
1. N *ga hoshii desu*
2. V *masu*-form *tai desu*
3. N (place) *e* { V *masu*-form / N } *ni ikimasu/kimasu/kaerimasu*
4. N *ni* V/N *o* V
5. *dokoka/nanika*
6. *go-chūmon*

LESSON 14 ··········· 90
I. Vocabulary
II. Translation
   Sentence Patterns & Example Sentences
   Conversation:
      To Umeda, please
III. Reference Words & Information:
   STATION

IV. Grammar Explanation
1. Verb conjugation
2. Verb groups
3. Verb *te*-form
4. V *te*-form *kudasai*
5. V *te*-form *imasu*
6. V *masu*-form *mashō ka*
7. S_1 *ga*, S_2
8. N *ga* V

LESSON 15 ··········· 96
I. Vocabulary
II. Translation
   Sentence Patterns & Example Sentences
   Conversation:
      Tell me about your family
III. Reference Words & Information:
   OCCUPATIONS

IV. Grammar Explanation
1. V *te*-form *mo ii desu*
2. V *te*-form *wa ikemasen*
3. V *te*-form *imasu*
4. V *te*-form *imasu*
5. *shirimasen*

LESSON 16 ··········· 102
I. Vocabulary
II. Translation
   Sentence Patterns & Example Sentences
   Conversation:
      Tell me how to use this machine
III. Reference Words & Information:
   HOW TO WITHDRAW MONEY

IV. Grammar Explanation
1. V *te*-form, [V *te*-form], ~
2. *i*-adj (~い) → ~*kute*, ~
3. N / *na*-adj [な] } *de*, ~
4. V_1 *te*-form *kara*, V_2
5. N_1 *wa* N_2 *ga* adjective
6. *dōyatte*
7. *dono* N

LESSON 17 · 108
I. Vocabulary
II. Translation
   Sentence Patterns & Example Sentences
   Conversation:
      What seems to be the problem?
III. Reference Words & Information:
   BODY & ILLNESS

IV. Grammar Explanation
1. Verb *nai*-form
2. V *nai*-form *nai de kudasai*
3. V *nai*-form *nakereba narimasen*
4. V *nai*-form *nakute mo ii desu*
5. N (object) *wa*
6. N (time) *made ni* V

LESSON 18 · 114
I. Vocabulary
II. Translation
   Sentence Patterns & Example Sentences
   Conversation:
      What is your hobby?
III. Reference Words & Information:
   ACTIONS

IV. Grammar Explanation
1. Verb dictionary form
2. $\left.\begin{array}{l}\text{N}\\ \text{V dictionary form } koto\end{array}\right\}$ *ga dekimasu*
3. *Watashi no shumi wa* $\left\{\begin{array}{l}\text{N}\\ \text{V dictionary form } koto\end{array}\right\}$ *desu*
4. $\left.\begin{array}{l}\text{V}_1 \text{ dictionary form}\\ \text{N } no\\ \text{Quantifier (period)}\end{array}\right\}$ *mae ni*, V$_2$
5. *nakanaka*
6. *zehi*

LESSON 19 · 120
I. Vocabulary
II. Translation
   Sentence Patterns & Example Sentences
   Conversation:
      As for my diet, I'll start it tomorrow
III. Reference Words & Information:
   TRADITIONAL CULTURE & ENTERTAINMENT

IV. Grammar Explanation
1. Verb *ta*-form
2. V *ta*-form *koto ga arimasu*
3. V *ta*-form *ri*, V *ta*-form *ri shimasu*
4. $\left.\begin{array}{l}i\text{-adj }(\sim\cancel{i}) \to \sim ku\\ na\text{-adj }[\cancel{na}] \to ni\\ \text{N } ni\end{array}\right\}$ *narimasu*
5. *Sō desu ne*

LESSON 20 · 126
I. Vocabulary
II. Translation
   Sentence Patterns & Example Sentences
   Conversation:
      What will you do for the summer vacation?
III. Reference Words & Information:
   HOW TO ADDRESS PEOPLE

IV. Grammar Explanation
1. Polite style and plain style
2. Proper use of the polite style or the plain style
3. Conversation in the plain style

LESSON 21 ·· 132

I. Vocabulary
II. Translation
    Sentence Patterns & Example Sentences
    Conversation:
        I think so, too
III. Reference Words & Information:
    POSITIONS IN SOCIETY

IV. Grammar Explanation
1. plain form *to omoimasu*
2. "S"
   plain form } *to iimasu*
3. V
   i-adj } plain form
   na-adj | plain form } *deshō?*
   N | ~*da*
4. N₁ (place) *de* N₂ *ga arimasu*
5. N (occasion) *de*
6. N *demo* V
7. V *nai*-form *nai to*······

LESSON 22 ·· 138

I. Vocabulary
II. Translation
    Sentence Patterns & Example Sentences
    Conversation:
        What kind of apartment would you like?
III. Reference Words & Information:
    CLOTHES

IV. Grammar Explanation
1. Noun modification
2. Noun modification by sentences
3. N *ga*
4. V dictionary form *jikan/yakusoku/ yōji*

LESSON 23 ·· 144

I. Vocabulary
II. Translation
    Sentence Patterns & Example Sentences
    Conversation:
        How can I get there?
III. Reference Words & Information:
    ROAD & TRAFFIC

IV. Grammar Explanation
1. V dictionary form
   V *nai*-form
   i-adj (~*i*) } *toki, ~*
   na-adj *na*
   N *no*
2. V dictionary form } *toki, ~*
   V *ta*-form
3. V dictionary form *to, ~*
4. N *ga* adjective/V
5. N (place) *o* V (verb of movement)

LESSON 24 · 150
I. Vocabulary
II. Translation
    Sentence Patterns & Example Sentences
    Conversation:
        Will you help me?
III. Reference Words & Information:
    EXCHANGE OF PRESENTS

IV. Grammar Explanation
    1. *kuremasu*
    2. V *te*-form { *agemasu* / *moraimasu* / *kuremasu* }
    3. N (person) *ga* V
    4. Interrogative *ga* V

LESSON 25 · 156
I. Vocabulary
II. Translation
    Sentence Patterns & Example Sentences
    Conversation:
        Thank you for having been kind to me
III. Reference Words & Information:
    LIFE

IV. Grammar Explanation
    1. plain past form *ra*, ~
    2. V *ta*-form *ra*, ~
    3. V *te*-form
       i-adj (~*i*) → ~*kute*
       na-adj [*na*] → *de*   } *mo*, ~
       N *de*
    4. *moshi* and *ikura*
    5. N *ga*

SUMMARY LESSON · 163
I. Particles
II. How to Use the Forms
III. Adverbs and Adverbial Expressions
IV. Various Conjunctions

APPENDICES · 172
I. Numerals
II. Expressions of time
III. Expressions of period
IV. Counters
V. Conjugation of verbs

INTRODUCTION

I. General Features of Japanese

1. Parts of Speech
The Japanese language is comprised of verbs, adjectives, nouns, adverbs, conjunctions and particles.

2. Word Order
A predicate always comes at the end of a sentence. A modifier always comes before the word or phrase to be modified.

3. Predicate
There are three types of predicates in Japanese: noun, verb and adjective. A predicate inflects according to whether it is (1) affirmative or negative and (2) non-past or past.

Adjectives are divided into two types according to their type of inflection. They are called *i*-adjectives and *na*-adjectives.

In Japanese, words do not inflect for person, gender or number.

4. Particle
A particle is used to show the grammatical relation between words, to show the speaker's intention or to connect sentences.

5. Omission
Words or phrases are often omitted if they are understood from the context. Even the subject and object of a sentence are often omitted.

II. Japanese Script

There are three kinds of letters in Japanese: hiragana, katakana and kanji (Chinese characters). Hiragana and katakana are phonetic representations of sounds, and each letter basically corresponds to one mora (a unit of sound. See Ⅲ). Kanji convey meanings as well as sounds.

In Japanese script, all three types of letters are used together. Katakana are used to write foreign names and loan words. 1945 kanji letters are fixed as essential for daily use. Hiragana are used to write particles, the inflectable parts of words, etc. Other than these three types of letters, romaji (Roman letters) are sometimes used for the convenience of foreigners. You may see romaji at stations and on signboards. Below are examples of all four types of script.

田中 さん は ミラー さん と デパート へ 行 きます。
○　　□　□　△　　　□　□　△　　　□　○　□

Mr. Tanaka is going to the department store with Mr. Miller.

大阪　　Osaka
○　　　☆

(○ – kanji　　□ – hiragana　　△ – katakana　　☆ – romaji)

III. Pronunciation of Japanese
1. Kana and Mora

e.g.,

	hiragana script
あ ア	katakana script
a	the Roman alphabet

	a-line	*i*-line	*u*-line	*e*-line	*o*-line
a-row	あ ア a	い イ i	う ウ u	え エ e	お オ o
ka-row k	か カ ka	き キ ki	く ク ku	け ケ ke	こ コ ko
sa-row s	さ サ sa	し シ shi	す ス su	せ セ se	そ ソ so
ta-row t	た タ ta	ち チ chi	つ ツ tsu	て テ te	と ト to
na-row n	な ナ na	に ニ ni	ぬ ヌ nu	ね ネ ne	の ノ no
ha-row h	は ハ ha	ひ ヒ hi	ふ フ fu	へ ヘ he	ほ ホ ho
ma-row m	ま マ ma	み ミ mi	む ム mu	め メ me	も モ mo
ya-row y	や ヤ ya	(い イ) (i)	ゆ ユ yu	(え エ) (e)	よ ヨ yo
ra-row r	ら ラ ra	り リ ri	る ル ru	れ レ re	ろ ロ ro
wa-row w	わ ワ wa	(い イ) (i)	(う ウ) (u)	(え エ) (e)	を ヲ o
	ん ン n				

きゃ キャ kya	きゅ キュ kyu	きょ キョ kyo
しゃ シャ sha	しゅ シュ shu	しょ ショ sho
ちゃ チャ cha	ちゅ チュ chu	ちょ チョ cho
にゃ ニャ nya	にゅ ニュ nyu	にょ ニョ nyo
ひゃ ヒャ hya	ひゅ ヒュ hyu	ひょ ヒョ hyo
みゃ ミャ mya	みゅ ミュ myu	みょ ミョ myo

りゃ リャ rya	りゅ リュ ryu	りょ リョ ryo

ga-row g	が ガ ga	ぎ ギ gi	ぐ グ gu	げ ゲ ge	ご ゴ go
za-row z	ざ ザ za	じ ジ ji	ず ズ zu	ぜ ゼ ze	ぞ ゾ zo
da-row d	だ ダ da	ぢ ヂ ji	づ ヅ zu	で デ de	ど ド do
ba-row b	ば バ ba	び ビ bi	ぶ ブ bu	べ ベ be	ぼ ボ bo
pa-row p	ぱ パ pa	ぴ ピ pi	ぷ プ pu	ぺ ペ pe	ぽ ポ po

ぎゃ ギャ gya	ぎゅ ギュ gyu	ぎょ ギョ gyo
じゃ ジャ ja	じゅ ジュ ju	じょ ジョ jo
びゃ ビャ bya	びゅ ビュ byu	びょ ビョ byo
ぴゃ ピャ pya	ぴゅ ピュ pyu	ぴょ ピョ pyo

The katakana letters in the square on the right are not in the above table. They are used to write sounds which are not original Japanese sounds but are needed for use in loan words.

	ウィ wi		ウェ we	ウォ wo
			シェ she	
			チェ che	
ツァ tsa			ツェ tse	ツォ tso
	ティ ti	トゥ tu		
ファ fa	フィ fi		フェ fe	フォ fo
			ジェ je	
	ディ di	ドゥ du		
		デュ dyu		

The Japanese language is based on five vowel sounds: *a, i, u, e* and *o* (see the table on the previous page). All spoken sounds are derived from these five vowels. They are used alone or are attached to either a consonant (e.g., k + a = *ka*) or a consonant plus the semi-vowel "y" (e.g., k + y + a = *kya*). The exception to this is a special mora, *n*, which is not followed by vowels. All of these sounds are of equal length when spoken.

[Note] A mora is a unit of sound in Japanese.

2. Long Vowels

A long vowel is pronounced twice as long as the ordinary vowels *a, i, u, e* and *o*. If you count the length of the vowel *a* as one, the length of the long vowel *ā* is counted as two. This means *a* is one mora long, whereas *ā* is two moras long.

Whether a vowel is long or not can change the meaning of the word.

e.g., obasan (aunt) : obāsan (grandmother)
ojisan (uncle) : ojiisan (grandfather)
yuki (snow) : yūki (courage)
e (picture) : ē (yes)   toru (take) : tōru (pass)
koko (here) : kōkō (high school)   heya (room) : heiya (plain)
kādo (card)   takushii (taxi)   sūpā (supermarket)
tēpu (tape)   nōto (notebook)

[Note]

How to write the long vowels in *rōmaji*

In romanized transcription (*rōmaji*), a long vowel is marked by a bar above the letter as shown below, except for the long vowels of *i* and *e* which are written as *ii* and *ei*.

short vowel : a   i   u   e   o
long vowel : ā   ii   ū   ei   ō

* *ē* is used in some words such as :
   ē (yes)   nē (say)   onēsan (older sister)

* *ē* is also used to write loan words :
   kēki (cake)

3. Pronunciation of n

n never appears at the beginning of a word. It constitutes one mora. For easier pronunciation, the way it is said changes according to the sound that comes after it.

1) It is pronounced /n/ before the sounds in the *ta*-, *da*-, *ra*- and *na*-rows.

   e.g., hantai (opposite) undō (sport) senro (rail) minna (all)

2) It is pronounced /m/ before the sounds in the *ba*-, *pa*- and *ma*-rows.

   e.g., shinbun (newspaper) enpitsu (pencil) unmei (destiny)

3) It is pronounced /ŋ/ before the sounds in the *ka*- and *ga*-rows.

   e.g., tenki (weather) kengaku (visit)

4. Double Consonants

Some consonants such as k, s, t and p occur as double consonants. In writing loan words, z and d also occur as double consonants.

   e.g., buka (subordinate) : bukka (commodity price)
   kasai (fire) : kassai (applause)
   oto (sound) : otto (husband)
   nikki (diary) zasshi (magazine) kitte (stamp)
   ippai (a cup of ~) koppu (glass) beddo (bed)

5. Consonant + ya, yu, yo

Such sounds as *kya, kyu, kyo* and *gya, gyu, gyo* are counted as one mora sound.

   e.g., hyaku (hundred)   (hya-ku : 2 moras)
   hiyaku (jump)   (hi-ya-ku : 3 moras)

6. Pronunciation of the *ga*-row

The consonant of this row, when it comes at the beginning of a word, is pronounced [g]. In other cases, it is usually pronounced [ŋ]. Recently some Japanese do not differentiate between [g] and [ŋ], and always use [g].

7. Devoicing of Vowels [i] and [u]

The vowels [i] and [u] are devoiced and not heard when they come between voiceless consonants. The vowel [u] of [su] in ~desu or ~masu is also devoiced when the sentence finishes with either ~desu or ~masu.

eg., s*u*ki (like)   sh*i*tai des*u* (want to do)   k*i*kimas*u* (listen)

8. Accent

The Japanese language has pitch accent. That is, some moras in a word are pronounced high and others low. The words are divided into two types according to whether a word has a falling pitch or not. Words with a falling pitch are subdivided into three types according to where the fall in pitch occurs. The standard Japanese accent is characterized by the fact that the first and the second moras have different pitches, and that the pitch never rises again once it has fallen.

[Types of Accent]

1) A fall in pitch does not occur. 　　　　　　　　　　　　　[⎡‾‾]

   e.g., niwa (garden)   hana (bise)   namae (name)   Nihon-go (Japanese language)

2) A fall in pitch comes after the first mora. 　　　　　　　[‾⎤_]

   e.g., hon (book)   tenki (weather)   raigetsu (next month)

3) A fall in pitch comes in the word at some place after the second mora. [⎡‾⎤_]

   e.g., tamago (egg)   hikōki [hikooki] (airplane)   sensei (teacher)

4) A fall in pitch comes after the last mora. 　　　　　　　　[⎡‾‾]]

   e.g., kutsu (shoes)   hana (flower)   yasumi (holiday)   otōto (younger brother)

"hana (nose)" in 1) and "hana (flower)" in 4) are alike, but the type of accent is different, because if a particle like *ga* is added after each word 1) is pronounced hana ga, whereas 4) is pronounced hana ga. The following are some other examples of words whose meaning differ according to the type of accent.

e.g., hashi (bridge) : hashi (chopsticks)   ichi (one) : ichi (location)

There are local differences in accent. For example, the accent of the area around Osaka is quite different from the standard one. The following are examples.

e.g., 　　　　Tokyo accent　　:　Osaka accent
　　(standard Japanese accent)
　　　　　　　　　　hana　　:　hana　　(flower)
　　　　　　　　　　ringo　　:　ringo　　(apple)
　　　　　　　　　　ongaku　:　ongaku　(music)

9. Intonation

There are three patterns. They are 1) flat, 2) rising and 3) falling. Questions are pronounced with a rising intonation. Other sentences are usually pronounced flat, but sometimes with a falling intonation. A falling intonation can express feelings such as agreement or disappointment, etc.

e.g., Satō : *Ashita tomodachi to o-hanami o shimasu.* 【→ flat】
 Mirā-san mo issho ni ikimasen ka. 【↗ rising】
Mirā : *Ā, ii desu nē.* 【↘ falling】
Sato : I'll go to see the cherry blossoms with my friends tomorrow. Won't you come with us, Mr. Miller?
Miller: Oh, that sounds good.

PRELIMINARY LESSON

I. Pronunciation

1. Kana and Mora

2. Long Vowels
obasan (aunt) : obāsan (grandmother)
ojisan (uncle) : ojiisan (grandfather)
yuki (snow) : yūki (courage)
e (picture) : ē (yes)   toru (take) : tōru (pass)
koko (here) : kōkō (high school)   heya (room) : heiya (plain)
kādo (card)   takushii (taxi)   sūpā (supermarket)
tēpu (tape)   nōto (notebook)

3. Pronunciation of *n*
enpitsu (pencil)   minna (all)   tenki (weather)   kin'en (no smoking)

4. Pronunciation of double consonants
buka (subordinate) : bukka (commodity price)
kasai (fire) : kassai (applause)
oto (sound) : otto (husband)
nikki (diary)   zasshi (magazine)   kitte (stamp)
ippai (a cup of ~)   koppu (glass)   beddo (bed)

5. Pronunciation of *"yōon"*
hiyaku (jump) : hyaku (hundred)
jiyū (freedom) : jū (ten)
biyōin (beauty parlor) : byōin (hospital)
shatsu (shirt)   ocha (tea)   gyūnyū (milk)
kyō (today)   buchō (department chief)   ryokō (travel)

6. Accent
niwa (garden)   namae (name)   Nihon-go (Japanese language)
hon (book)   tenki (weather)   raigetsu (next month)
tamago (egg)   hikōki [hikooki] (airplane)   sensei (teacher)
kutsu (shoes)   yasumi (holiday)   otōto (younger brother)
hashi (bridge) : hashi (chopsticks)   ichi (one) : ichi (location)

      e.g.,   Tokyo accent   :   Osaka accent
    (standard Japanese accent)

                      hana   :   hana   (flower)
                      ringo   :   ringo   (apple)
                      ōngaku :   ongaku (music)

7. Intonation

    e.g., *Satō* : *Ashita tomodachi to o-hanami o shimasu.* 【→ flat】
                 Mirā-san mo issho ni ikimasen ka. 【↗ rising】
      Mirā : *Ā, ii desu nē.* 【↘ falling】
      Sato : I'll go to see the cherry blossoms with my friends tomorrow. Won't you come with us, Mr. Miller?
      Miller : Oh, that sounds good.

II. Classroom Instructions

1. Let's begin.
2. Let's finish (the lesson).
3. Let's take a break.
4. Do you understand? (Yes, I do./No, I don't.)
5. Once more.
6. Fine. / Good.
7. That's not OK. / That's wrong.
8. name
9. exam, homework
10. question, answer, example

III. Daily Greetings and Expressions

1. Good morning.
2. Good afternoon.
3. Good evening.
4. Good night.
5. Good-bye.
6. Thank you very much.
7. Excuse me. / I'm sorry.
8. Please.

IV. Numerals

0   zero
1   one
2   two
3   three
4   four
5   five
6   six
7   seven
8   eight
9   nine
10 ten

TERMS USED FOR INSTRUCTION

dai – ka	lesson –	meishi	noun
bunkei	sentence pattern	dōshi	verb
reibun	example sentence	keiyōshi	adjective
kaiwa	conversation	i-keiyōshi	*i*-adjective
renshū	practice	na-keiyōshi	*na*-adjective
mondai	exercise	joshi	particle
kotae	answer	fukushi	adverb
yomimono	reading practice	setsuzokushi	conjunction
fukushū	review	sūshi	quantifier
		josūshi	counters
mokuji	contents	gimonshi	interrogative (question word)
sakuin	index		
		meishi-bun	noun (predicate) sentence
bunpō	grammar	dōshi-bun	verb (predicate) sentence
bun	sentence	keiyōshi-bun	adjective (predicate) sentence
tango (go)	word		
ku	phrase	shugo	subject
setsu	clause	jutsugo	predicate
		mokutekigo	object
hatsuon	pronunciation	shudai	topic
boin	vowel		
shiin	consonant	kōtei	affirmative
haku	mora	hitei	negative
akusento	accent	kanryō	perfective
intonēshon	intonation	mi-kanryō	imperfective
		kako	past
[ka-] gyō	[*ka*-]row	hi-kako	non-past
[i-] retsu	[*i*-]line		

teinei-tai	polite style of speech
futsū-tai	plain style of speech
katsuyō	inflection
fōmu	form
~kei	~form
shūshoku	modification
reigai	exception

ABBREVIATIONS

N   noun （meishi）
- e.g., gakusei   tsukue
-        student   desk

i-adj   *i*-adjective （i-keiyōshi）
- e.g., oishii   takai
-        tasty   high

na-adj   *na*-adjective （na-keiyōshi）
- e.g., kirei [na]   shizuka [na]
-        beautiful   quiet

V   verb （dōshi）
- e.g., kakimasu   tabemasu
-        write   eat

S   sentence （bun）
- e.g., Kore wa hon desu.
-        This is a book.
-        Watashi wa ashita Tōkyō e ikimasu.
-        I will go to Tokyo tomorrow.

Lesson 1

I. Vocabulary

watashi	わたし	I
watashitachi	わたしたち	we
anata	あなた	you
ano hito	あの ひと	that person, he, she
(ano kata)	(あの かた)	(*ano kata* is the polite equivalent of *ano hito*)
minasan	みなさん	ladies and gentlemen, all of you
~san	~さん	Mr., Ms. (title of respect added to a name)
~chan	~ちゃん	(suffix often added to a child's name instead of ~*san*)
~kun	~くん	(suffix often added to a boy's name)
~jin	~じん	(suffix meaning "a national of"; e.g., *Amerika-jin*, an American)
sensei	せんせい	teacher, instructor (not used when referring to one's own job)
kyōshi	きょうし	teacher, instructor
gakusei	がくせい	student
kaishain	かいしゃいん	company employee
shain	しゃいん	employee of ~ Company (used with a company's name; e.g., *IMC no shain*)
ginkōin	ぎんこういん	bank employee
isha	いしゃ	medical doctor
kenkyūsha	けんきゅうしゃ	researcher, scholar
enjinia	エンジニア	engineer
daigaku	だいがく	university
byōin	びょういん	hospital
denki	でんき	electricity, light
dare (donata)	だれ (どなた)	who (*donata* is the polite equivalent of *dare*)

－sai	－さい	－ years old
nan-sai (o-ikutsu)	なんさい (おいくつ)	how old (*o-ikutsu* is the polite equivalent of *nan-sai*)
hai	はい	yes
iie	いいえ	no
shitsurei desu ga	しつれいですが	Excuse me, but
O-namae wa?	おなまえは？	May I have your name?
Hajimemashite.	はじめまして。	How do you do? (lit. I am meeting you for the first time. Usually used as the first phrase when introducing oneself.)
Dōzo yoroshiku [onegai-shimasu].	どうぞ よろしく ［おねがいします］。	Pleased to meet you. (lit. Please be nice to me. Usually used at the end of a self-introduction.)
Kochira wa ～san desu.	こちらは ～さんです。	This is Mr./Ms.～.
～ kara kimashita.	～から きました	I came (come) from ～.

Amerika	アメリカ	U.S.A.
Igirisu	イギリス	U.K.
Indo	インド	India
Indoneshia	インドネシア	Indonesia
Kankoku	かんこく	South Korea
Tai	タイ	Thailand
Chūgoku	ちゅうごく	China
Doitsu	ドイツ	Germany
Nihon	にほん	Japan
Furansu	フランス	France
Burajiru	ブラジル	Brazil
Sakura-daigaku/ Fuji-daigaku	さくらだいがく／ ふじだいがく	fictitious universities
IMC/Pawā-denki/ Burajiru-eā	IMC／パワーでんき／ ブラジルエアー	fictitious companies
AKC	AKC	fictitious institute
Kōbe-byōin	こうべびょういん	fictitious hospital

II. Translation

Sentence Patterns

1. I am Mike Miller.
2. Mr. Santos is not a student.
3. Is Mr. Miller a company employee?
4. Mr. Santos is also a company employee.

Example Sentences

1. Are you Mr. Mike Miller?
   ···Yes, I am Mike Miller.

2. Are you a student, Mr. Miller?
   ···No, I am not a student.
   I am a company employee.

3. Is Mr. Wang an engineer?
   ···No, Mr. Wang is not an engineer.
   He is a doctor.

4. Who is that person?
   ···He is Professor Watt. He is a teacher at Sakura University.

5. How old is Teresa?
   ···She is nine years old.

Conversation

How do you do?

Sato:	Good morning.
Yamada:	Good morning.
	Ms. Sato, this is Mr. Mike Miller.
Miller:	How do you do? I am Mike Miller.
	I am from the United States of America.
	Nice to meet you.
Sato:	I am Sato Keiko.
	Nice to meet you.

III. Reference Words & Information

KUNI · HITO · KOTOBA COUNTRY, PEOPLE & LANGUAGE

Kuni Country	Hito People	Kotoba Language
Amerika (U.S.A.)	Amerika-jin	Eigo (English)
Igirisu (U.K.)	Igirisu-jin	Eigo (English)
Itaria (Italy)	Itaria-jin	Itaria-go (Italian)
Iran (Iran)	Iran-jin	Perusha-go (Persian)
Indo (India)	Indo-jin	Hindii-go (Hindi)
Indoneshia (Indonesia)	Indoneshia-jin	Indoneshia-go (Indonesian)
Ejiputo (Egypt)	Ejiputo-jin	Arabia-go (Arabic)
Ōsutoraria (Australia)	Ōsutoraria-jin	Eigo (English)
Kanada (Canada)	Kanada-jin	Eigo (English) Furansu-go (French)
Kankoku (South Korea)	Kankoku-jin	Kankoku-go (Korean)
Saujiarabia (Saudi Arabia)	Saujiarabia-jin	Arabia-go (Arabic)
Shingapōru (Singapore)	Shingapōru-jin	Eigo (English)
Supein (Spain)	Supein-jin	Supein-go (Spanish)
Tai (Thailand)	Tai-jin	Tai-go (Thai)
Chūgoku (China)	Chūgoku-jin	Chūgoku-go (Chinese)
Doitsu (Germany)	Doitsu-jin	Doitsu-go (German)
Nihon (Japan)	Nihon-jin	Nihon-go (Japanese)
Furansu (France)	Furansu-jin	Furansu-go (French)
Firipin (Philippines)	Firipin-jin	Firipino-go (Filipino)
Burajiru (Brazil)	Burajiru-jin	Porutogaru-go (Portuguese)
Betonamu (Vietnam)	Betonamu-jin	Betonamu-go (Vietnamese)
Marēshia (Malaysia)	Marēshia-jin	Marēshia-go (Malaysian)
Mekishiko (Mexico)	Mekishiko-jin	Supein-go (Spanish)
Roshia (Russia)	Roshia-jin	Roshia-go (Russian)

IV. Grammar Explanation

1. $\boxed{N_1 \text{ wa } N_2 \text{ } desu}$

   1) Particle *wa*

   The particle *wa* indicates that the word before it is the topic of the sentence. You select a noun you want to talk about, add *wa* to show that it is the topic and give a statement about the topic.

   ① Watashi wa Maiku Mirā desu.　　　　I am Mike Miller.

   2) *desu*

   Nouns used with *desu* work as predicates.
   desu indicates judgement or assertion.
   desu also conveys that the speaker is being polite towards the listener.
   desu inflects when the sentence is negative (see 2. below) or in the past tense (see Lesson 12).

   ② Watashi wa enjinia desu.　　　　　I am an engineer.

2. $\boxed{N_1 \text{ wa } N_2 \text{ } ja \text{ } arimasen}$

   ja arimasen is the negative form of *desu*. It is the form used in daily conversation. For a formal speech or writing, *dewa arimasen* is used instead.

   ③ Santosu-san wa gakusei ja arimasen.　　Mr. Santos is not a student.
   　　　　　　　　　(dewa)

3. $\boxed{S \text{ } ka}$

   1) Particle *ka*

   The particle *ka* is used to express the speaker's doubt, question, uncertainty, etc. A question is formed by simply adding *ka* to the end of the sentence. A question ends with a rising intonation.

   2) Questions asking whether a statement is correct or not

   As mentioned above, a sentence becomes a question when *ka* is added to the end. The word order does not change. The question thus made asks whether a statement is correct or not. Depending on whether you agree with the statement or not, your answer to such a question begins with *hai* or *iie*.

   ④ Mirā-san wa Amerika-jin desu ka.　　Is Mr. Miller an American?
   　　⋯Hai, Amerika-jin desu.　　　　　⋯Yes, he is.

   ⑤ Mirā-san wa sensei desu ka.　　　　Is Mr. Miller a teacher?
   　　⋯Iie, sensei ja arimasen.　　　　　⋯No, he is not.

   3) Questions with interrogatives

   An interrogative replaces the part of the sentence that covers what you want to ask about. The word order does not change, and *ka* is added at the end.

   ⑥ Ano kata wa donata desu ka.　　　　Who is that man?
   　　⋯[Ano kata wa] Mirā-san desu.　　⋯That's Mr. Miller.

4. N *mo*

mo is added after a topic instead of *wa* when the statement about the topic is the same as the previous topic.

⑦ Mirā-san wa kaishain desu.   Mr. Miller is a company employee.

   Guputa-san mo kaishain desu.   Mr. Gupta is also a company employee.

5. N₁ *no* N₂

no is used to connect two nouns. N₁ modifies N₂. In Lesson 1, N₁ is an organization or some kind of group to which N₂ belongs.

⑧ Mirā-san wa IMC no shain desu.   Mr. Miller is an IMC employee.

6. ~ *san*

san is added to the name of the listener or a third person to show the speaker's respect to the person. It should never be used with the speaker's own name.

⑨ Ano kata wa Mirā-san desu.   That's Mr. Miller.

When referring directly to the listener, the word *anata* (you) is not commonly used if you know the listener's name. The listener's family name followed by *san* is usually used.

⑩ Suzuki : Mirā-san wa gakusei desu ka.

   Mirā : Iie, kaishain desu.

   Suzuki : Are you a student?

   Miller : No, I'm a company employee.

Lesson 2

I. Vocabulary

kore	これ	this (thing here)
sore	それ	that (thing near you)
are	あれ	that (thing over there)
kono ~	この ~	this ~, this ~ here
sono ~	その ~	that ~, that ~ near you
ano ~	あの ~	that ~, that ~ over there
hon	ほん	book
jisho	じしょ	dictionary
zasshi	ざっし	magazine
shinbun	しんぶん	newspaper
nōto	ノート	notebook
techō	てちょう	pocket notebook
meishi	めいし	business card
kādo	カード	card
terehon-kādo	テレホンカード	telephone card
enpitsu	えんぴつ	pencil
bōrupen	ボールペン	ballpoint pen
shāpu-penshiru	シャープペンシル	mechanical pencil, propelling pencil
kagi	かぎ	key
tokei	とけい	watch, clock
kasa	かさ	umbrella
kaban	かばん	bag, briefcase
[kasetto-]tēpu	[カセット]テープ	[cassette] tape
tēpu-rekōdā	テープレコーダー	tape recorder
terebi	テレビ	television
rajio	ラジオ	radio
kamera	カメラ	camera
konpyūtā	コンピューター	computer
jidōsha	じどうしゃ	automobile, car

tsukue	つくえ	desk
isu	いす	chair
chokorēto	チョコレート	chocolate
kōhii	コーヒー	coffee
Eigo	えいご	the English language
Nihon-go	にほんご	the Japanese language
～go	～ご	～ language
nan	なん	what
sō	そう	so
Chigaimasu.	ちがいます。	No, it isn't./You are wrong.
Sō desu ka.	そうですか。	I see./Is that so?
anō	あのう	well (used to show hesitation)
Honno kimochi desu.	ほんの きもちです。	It's nothing./It's a token of my gratitude.
Dōzo.	どうぞ。	Please./Here you are. (used when offering someone something)
Dōmo.	どうも。	Well, thanks.
[Dōmo] arigatō [gozaimasu].	[どうも] ありがとう [ございます]。	Thank you [very much].

◁ Kaiwa ▷

Korekara osewa ni narimasu.	これから おせわに なります。	I hope for your kind assistance hereafter.
Kochira koso yoroshiku.	こちらこそ よろしく。	I am pleased to meet you. (response to *Dōzo yoroshiku*)

II. Translation

Sentence Patterns

1. This is a dictionary.
2. This is a book on computers.
3. That is my umbrella.
4. This umbrella is mine.

Example Sentences

1. Is this a telephone card?
   ···Yes, it is.
2. Is that a notebook?
   ···No, it's not. It's a pocket notebook.
3. What is that?
   ···This is a business card.
4. Is this a "9" or a "7"?
   ···It's a "9."
5. What is that magazine about?
   ···It's a magazine on cars.
6. Whose bag is that?
   ···It's Ms. Sato's bag.
7. Is this umbrella yours?
   ···No, it's not mine.
8. Whose is this key?
   ···It's mine.

Conversation

This is just a token

Yamada:	Yes. Who is it?
Santos:	I am Santos from (apartment) 408.
	--
Santos:	Hello. I am Santos.
	How do you do?
	It is nice to meet you.
Yamada:	The pleasure's mine.
Santos:	Er, this is a little something...
Yamada:	Oh, thank you. What is it?
Santos:	It's coffee. Please.
Yamada:	Thank you very much.

III. Reference Words & Information

NAMAE   FAMILY NAMES

Most Common Family Names

1	Satō	2	Suzuki	3	Takahashi	4	Tanaka
5	Watanabe	6	Itō	7	Nakamura	8	Yamamoto
9	Kobayashi	10	Saitō	11	Katō	12	Yoshida
13	Yamada	14	Sasaki	15	Matsumoto	16	Yamaguchi
17	Kimura	18	Inoue	19	Abe	20	Hayashi

Greetings

"Hajimemashite."

⇐ When people meet for the first time on business, business cards are exchanged.

"Honno kimochi desu."

When you move house, it is polite to introduce yourself to your new neighbours and give them a small gift, such as a towel, soap or sweets. ⇨

IV. Grammar Explanation

1. *kore/sore/are*

kore, *sore* and *are* are demonstratives.
   They work as nouns. *kore* refers to a thing near the speaker. *sore* refers to a thing near the listener. *are* refers to a thing far from the speaker and the listener.

① Sore wa jisho desu ka. Is that a dictionary?
② Kore o kudasai. I'll take this. (lit. Please give this to me.)(L. 3)

2. *kono* N/*sono* N/*ano* N

kono, *sono* and *ano* modify nouns. "*kono* N" refers to a thing or a person near the speaker. "*sono* N" refers to a thing or a person near the listener. "*ano* N" refers to a thing or a person far from both the speaker and the listener.

③ Kono hon wa watashi no desu. This book is mine.
④ Ano kata wa donata desu ka. Who is that [person]?

kore kono kaban	sore sono kaban	are ano kaban

3. *sō desu/sō ja arimasen*

In the case of a noun sentence, the word *sō* is often used to answer a question requiring an affirmative or negative answer. *hai, sō desu* is the affirmative answer and *iie, sō ja arimasen* is the negative answer.

⑤ Sore wa terehon-kādo desu ka. Is that a telephone card?
   ···Hai, sō desu. ···Yes, it is. (lit. Yes, it's so.)
⑥ Sore wa terehon-kādo desu ka. Is that a telephone card?
   ···Iie, sō ja arimasen. ···No, it isn't. (lit. No, it's not so.)

The verb *chigaimasu* (lit. to differ) can be used to mean *sō ja arimasen*.

⑦ Sore wa terehon-kādo desu ka. Is that a telephone card?
   ···Iie, chigaimasu. ···No, it isn't.

4. S_1 *ka*, S_2 *ka*

This is a question asking the listener to choose between alternatives, S_1 and S_2, for the answer. As an answer to this type of question, the chosen sentence is stated. Neither *hai* nor *iie* is used.

⑧ Kore wa "9" desu ka, "7" desu ka.　　　Is this a "9" or a "7"?
　…"9" desu.　　　…It's a "9."

5. N_1 *no* N_2

You learned in Lesson 1 that *no* is used to connect two nouns when N_1 modifies N_2. In Lesson 2 you learn two other uses of this *no*.

1) N_1 explains what N_2 is about.

⑨ Kore wa konpyūtā no hon desu.　　　This is a book on computers.

2) N_1 explains who owns N_2.

⑩ Kore wa watashi no hon desu.　　　This is my book.

N_2 is sometimes omitted when it is obvious. When N_2 means a person, however, you cannot omit it.

⑪ Are wa dare no kaban desu ka.　　　Whose bag is that?
　…Satō-san no desu.　　　…It's Ms. Satō's.
⑫ Kono kaban wa anata no desu ka.　　　Is this bag yours?
　…Iie, watashi no ja arimasen.　　　…No, it's not mine.
⑬ Mirā-san wa IMC no shain desu ka.
　…Hai, IMC no shain desu.
　Is Mr. Miller an employee of IMC?
　…Yes, he is.

6. *Sō desu ka*

This expression is used when the speaker receives new information and shows that he or she understands it.

⑭ Kono kasa wa anata no desu ka.
　…Iie, chigaimasu. Shumitto-san no desu.
　Sō desu ka.
　Is this umbrella yours?
　…No, it's Mr. Schmidt's.
　I see.

Lesson 3

I. Vocabulary

koko	ここ	here, this place
soko	そこ	there, that place near you
asoko	あそこ	that place over there
doko	どこ	where, what place
kochira	こちら	this way, this place (polite equivalent of *koko*)
sochira	そちら	that way, that place near you (polite equivalent of *soko*)
achira	あちら	that way, that place over there (polite equivalent of *asoko*)
dochira	どちら	which way, where (polite equivalent of *doko*)
kyōshitsu	きょうしつ	classroom
shokudō	しょくどう	dining hall, canteen
jimusho	じむしょ	office
kaigishitsu	かいぎしつ	conference room, assembly room
uketsuke	うけつけ	reception desk
robii	ロビー	lobby
heya	へや	room
toire (otearai)	トイレ(おてあらい)	toilet, rest room
kaidan	かいだん	staircase
erebētā	エレベーター	elevator, lift
esukarētā	エスカレーター	escalator
[o-]kuni	[お]くに	country
kaisha	かいしゃ	company
uchi	うち	house, home
denwa	でんわ	telephone, telephone call
kutsu	くつ	shoes
nekutai	ネクタイ	necktie
wain	ワイン	wine
tabako	たばこ	tobacco, cigarette
uriba	うりば	department, counter (in a department store)

chika	ちか	basement
－kai (－gai)	－かい（－がい）	-th floor
nan-gai	なんがい	what floor
－en	－えん	－ yen
ikura	いくら	how much
hyaku	ひゃく	hundred
sen	せん	thousand
man	まん	ten thousand

◁ Kaiwa ▷

Sumimasen.	すみません。	Excuse me.
～ de gozaimasu.	～でございます。	(polite equivalent of *desu*)
[～ o] misete kudasai.	[～を] みせてください。	Please show me [～].
ja	じゃ	well, then, in that case
[～ o] kudasai.	[～を] ください。	Give me [～], please.

~~~~~~~~~~~~~~~~~~~~~~~~~~~~~~~~

Shin-Ōsaka	しんおおさか	name of a station in Osaka
Itaria	イタリア	Italy
Suisu	スイス	Switzerland
MT/Yōnen/Akikkusu	MT/ヨーネン/アキックス	fictitious companies

II. Translation

Sentence Patterns
1. This is a dining hall.
2. The telephone is over there.

Example Sentences
1. Is this Shin-Osaka?
   ···Yes, it is.
2. Where is the rest room?
   ···It is over there.
3. Where is Mr. Yamada?
   ···He is in the office.
4. Where is the elevator?
   ···It is there.
5. Which country are you from?
   ···America.
6. Where are those shoes from?
   ···They're Italian shoes.
7. How much is this watch?
   ···It's 18,600 yen.

Conversation

I'll take it

Maria:	Excuse me. Where is the wine department?
Sales clerk A:	It is in the first basement.
Maria:	Thanks.

Maria:	Excuse me. Could you show me that wine?
Sales clerk B:	Certainly. Here you are.
Maria:	Is this French wine?
Sales clerk B:	No, it's Italian.
Maria:	How much is it?
Sales clerk B:	2,500 yen.
Maria:	Well, I'll take it.

III. Reference Words & Information

DEPĀTO DEPARTMENT STORE

okujō	yūenchi amusement area	
8-kai	shokudō · moyōshimono-kaijō restaurants · event hall	
7-kai	tokei · megane · kamera watches · glasses · cameras	
6-kai	supōtsu-yōhin · ryokō-yōhin sporting goods · leisure goods	
5-kai	kodomo-fuku · omocha · hon · bunbōgu children's clothes · toys · books · stationery	
4-kai	kagu · shokki · denki-seihin furniture · kitchenware · electrical appliances	
3-gai	shinshi-fuku men's wear	
2-kai	fujin-fuku ladies' wear	
1-kai	kutsu · kaban · akusesarii · keshōhin shoes · bags · accessories · cosmetics	
B1-kai	shokuryōhin food	
B2-kai	chūshajō parking lot	

IV. Grammar Explanation

1. *koko/soko/asoko/kochira/sochira/achira*

   The demonstratives *kore*, *sore* and *are* that are discussed in Lesson 2 refer to a thing, while *koko*, *soko* and *asoko* refer to a place. *koko* is the place where the speaker is, *soko* is the place where the listener is, and *asoko* is the place far from both the speaker and the listener.

   kochira, *sochira* and *achira* are demonstrative words referring to direction. *kochira*, *sochira* and *achira* are also used to refer to location, in which case, they are politer than *koko*, *soko* and *asoko*.

   [Note] When the speaker regards the listener as sharing his/her territory, the place where they both are is designated by the word *koko*. Under this situation, *soko* designates the place a little distant from the speaker and listener, and *asoko* designates an even more distant location.

2. $\boxed{N_1 \ wa \ N_2(place) \ desu}$

   Using this sentence pattern, you can explain where a place, a thing or a person is.

   ① Otearai wa asoko desu.　　　The rest room is there.
   ② Denwa wa 2-kai desu.　　　The telephone is on the second floor.
   ③ Yamada-san wa jimusho desu.　Mr. Yamada is in the office.

3. *doko/dochira*

   doko means "where," and *dochira* means "which direction." *dochira* can also mean "where," in which case it's politer than *doko*.

   ④ Otearai wa doko desu ka.　　Where's the rest room?
   　…Asoko desu.　　　　　　…It's there.
   ⑤ Erebētā wa dochira desu ka.　Where's the elevator?
   　…Achira desu.　　　　　　…It's in that direction. (It's there.)

doko or *dochira* is also used to ask the name of a country, company, school or any place or organization a person belongs to. You cannot use *nan* (what). *dochira* is politer than *doko*.

⑥ Gakkō wa doko desu ka. What's the name of your school?

⑦ Kaisha wa dochira desu ka. What company do you work for?

4. N_1 *no* N_2

When N_1 is the name of a country and N_2 is a product, it means that N_2 is made in that country. When N_1 is the name of a company and N_2 is a product, it means that N_2 is made by that company. In this structure, *doko* is used to ask where or by whom N_2 is made.

⑧ Kore wa doko no konpyūta desu ka.
 ···Nihon no konpyūta desu.
 ···IMC no konpyūta desu.
 Where is this computer made?/ Who is the maker of this computer?
 ···It's made in Japan.
 ···IMC is.

5. The *ko/so/a/do* system of demonstrative words

	ko series	*so* series	*a* series	*do* series
thing	kore	sore	are	dore (L. 8)
thing person	kono N	sono N	ano N	dono N (L. 16)
place	koko	soko	asoko	doko
direction place (polite)	kochira	sochira	achira	dochira

6. *o-kuni*

The prefix *o* is added to a word concerning the listener or a third person in order to express the speaker's respect to the person.

⑨ [O-]kuni wa dochira desu ka. Where are you from?

Lesson 4

I. Vocabulary

okimasu	おきます	get up, wake up
nemasu	ねます	sleep, go to bed
hatarakimasu	はたらきます	work
yasumimasu	やすみます	take a rest, take a holiday
benkyō-shimasu	べんきょうします	study
owarimasu	おわります	finish
depāto	デパート	department store
ginkō	ぎんこう	bank
yūbinkyoku	ゆうびんきょく	post office
toshokan	としょかん	library
bijutsukan	びじゅつかん	art museum
ima	いま	now
－ji	－じ	－ o'clock
－fun (－pun)	－ふん（－ぶん）	－ minute
han	はん	half
nan-ji	なんじ	what time
nan-pun	なんぷん	what minute
gozen	ごぜん	a.m., morning
gogo	ごご	p.m., afternoon
asa	あさ	morning
hiru	ひる	daytime, noon
ban (yoru)	ばん（よる）	night, evening
ototoi	おととい	the day before yesterday
kinō	きのう	yesterday
kyō	きょう	today
ashita	あした	tomorrow
asatte	あさって	the day after tomorrow
kesa	けさ	this morning
konban	こんばん	this evening, tonight
yasumi	やすみ	rest, a holiday, a day off
hiruyasumi	ひるやすみ	lunchtime

maiasa	まいあさ	every morning
maiban	まいばん	every night
mainichi	まいにち	every day
getsu-yōbi	げつようび	Monday
ka-yōbi	かようび	Tuesday
sui-yōbi	すいようび	Wednesday
moku-yōbi	もくようび	Thursday
kin-yōbi	きんようび	Friday
do-yōbi	どようび	Saturday
nichi-yōbi	にちようび	Sunday
nan-yōbi	なんようび	what day of the week
bangō	ばんごう	number
nan-ban	なんばん	what number
～ kara	～から	from ～
～ made	～まで	up to ～, until ～
～ to ～	～と～	and (used to connect nouns)
sochira	そちら	your place
Taihen desu ne.	たいへんですね。	That's tough, isn't it? (used when expressing sympathy)
ēto	えーと	well, let me see

◁ Kaiwa ▷

104	１０４	information, directory assistance
Onegai-shimasu.	おねがいします。	Please. (lit. ask for a favor)
Kashikomarimashita.	かしこまりました。	Certainly (sir, madam).
o-toiawase no bangō	おといあわせのばんごう	the number being inquired about
[Dōmo] arigatō gozaimashita.	[どうも] ありがとう ございました。	Thank you very much.

Nyūyōku	ニューヨーク	New York
Pekin	ペキン	Beijing
Rondon	ロンドン	London
Bankoku	バンコク	Bangkok
Rosanzerusu	ロサンゼルス	Los Angeles
Yamato-bijutsukan	やまとびじゅつかん	fictitious art museum
Ōsaka-depāto	おおさかデパート	fictitious department store
Midori-toshokan	みどりとしょかん	fictitious library
Appuru-ginkō	アップルぎんこう	fictitious bank

II. Translation

Sentence Patterns

1. It is five past four now.
2. I work from nine to five.
3. I get up at six in the morning.
4. I studied yesterday.

Example Sentences

1. What time is it now?
   ···It is ten past two.
   What time is it now in New York?
   ···It is ten past twelve at night.

2. From what time to what time is the bank open?
   ···It is open from nine till three.
   On what day of the week is it closed?
   ···It is closed on Saturdays and Sundays.

3. What time do you go to bed every night?
   ···I go to bed at eleven o'clock.

4. Do you work on Saturdays?
   ···No, I don't.

5. Did you study yesterday?
   ···No, I didn't.

6. What is the telephone number of IMC?
   ···It is 341-2597.

Conversation

What are your opening hours?

104:	Hello, this is Ishida of the 104 Service.
Karina:	Could you tell me the phone number of the Yamato Art Museum, please?
104:	The Yamato Art Museum? Certainly.
-----	-----
Tape:	The number you are inquiring about is 0797-38-5432.
-----	-----
Museum staff member:	Hello, Yamato Art Museum.
Karina:	Excuse me. What are your opening hours?
Staff:	We are open from nine to four.
Karina:	Which day of the week are you closed?
Staff:	We are closed on Mondays.
Karina:	Thank you very much.

III. Reference Words & Information

DENWA · TEGAMI   PHONE & LETTER

How to Use a Public Phone

① Lift the receiver.
② Put coin or card into slot.
③ Press the numbers.
④ Hang up the receiver.
⑤ Take card or change if any.

Public phones accept only ¥10 coins, ¥100 coins, and telephone cards.
If you put in a ¥100 coin, no change will be returned.
* If the machine has a start button, press it after ③.

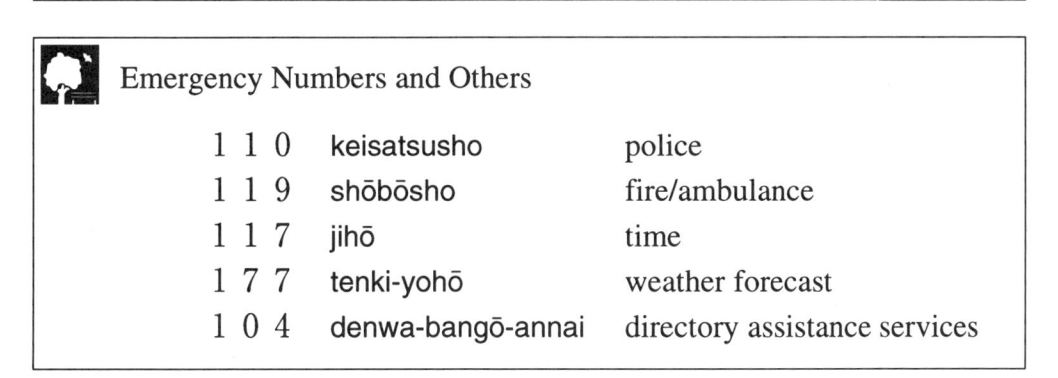

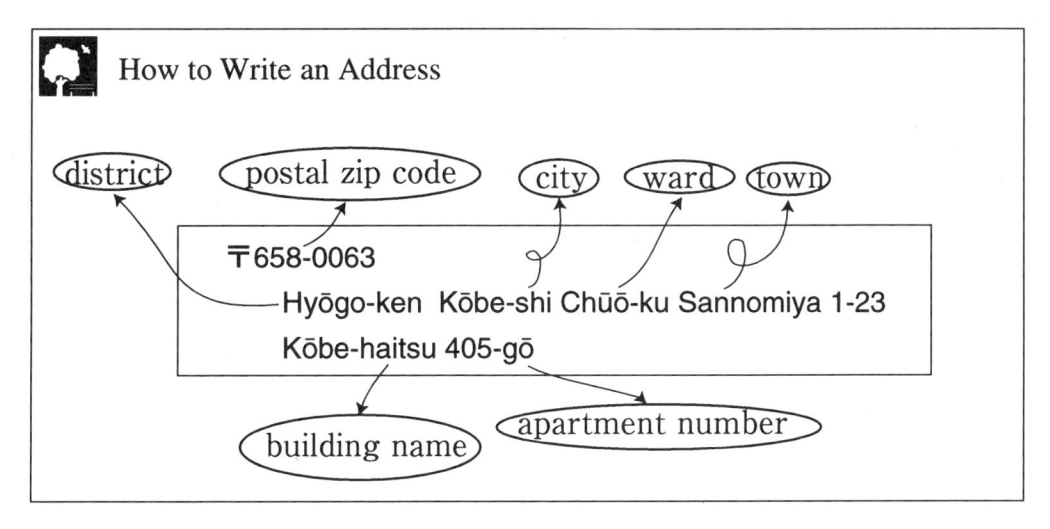

Emergency Numbers and Others

1 1 0	keisatsusho	police
1 1 9	shōbōsho	fire/ambulance
1 1 7	jihō	time
1 7 7	tenki-yohō	weather forecast
1 0 4	denwa-bangō-annai	directory assistance services

How to Write an Address

(district) (postal zip code) (city) (ward) (town)

〒658-0063
Hyōgo-ken Kōbe-shi Chūo-ku Sannomiya 1-23
Kōbe-haitsu 405-gō

(building name) (apartment number)

IV. Grammar Explanation

1. **Ima -ji -fun desu**

    To express time, the counter suffixes -ji (o'clock) and -fun(-pun) (minutes) are used. The numbers are put before them. -fun is used after 2, 5, 7 or 9 and -pun after 1, 3, 4, 6, 8 or 10. 1, 6, 8 and 10 are read ip(-pun), rop(-pun), hap(-pun) and jup/jip(-pun). (See Appendices II.)
    The interrogative *nan* is used with a counter suffix to ask questions concerning number or amounts. Therefore, the word *nan-ji* (or sometimes *nan-pun*) is used to ask the time.

    ① Ima nan-ji desu ka.   What time is it now?
    　…7-ji 10-pun desu.   …It's seven ten.

    [Note] *wa* marks the topic of a sentence, which you learned in Lesson 1. A geographical location can also be used as the topic as can be seen in ②.

    ② Nyūyōku wa ima nan-ji desu ka.   In New York what time is it now?
    　…Gozen 4-ji desu.   …It's 4 a.m.

2. **V-masu**

    1) A verb with *masu* works as a predicate.
    2) *masu* makes a sentence polite.

    ③ Watashi wa mainichi benkyō-shimasu.   I study every day.

3. **V-masu/ V-masen/ V-mashita/ V-masendeshita**

    1) *masu* is used when a sentence expresses a habitual thing or a truth. It is also used when a sentence expresses a thing that will occur in the future. The negative form and the forms in the past tense are shown in the table below.

	non-past (future/present)	past
affirmative	(oki) masu	(oki) mashita
negative	(oki) masen	(oki) masendeshita

    ④ Maiasa 6-ji ni okimasu.   I get up at six every morning.
    ⑤ Ashita 6-ji ni okimasu.   I'll get up at six tomorrow morning.
    ⑥ Kesa 6-ji ni okimashita.   I got up at six this morning.

    2) Question forms of verb sentences are made in the same way as those of noun sentences; i.e., the word order remains the same and *ka* is added to the end of the sentence.
    In answering such questions, the verbs in the questions are repeated. *sō desu* or *sō ja arimasen* (see Lesson 2) cannot be used.

    ⑦ Kinō benkyō-shimashita ka.   Did you study yesterday?
    　…Hai, benkyō-shimashita.   …Yes, I did.
    　…Iie, benkyō-shimasendeshita.   …No, I didn't.

⑧ Maiasa nan-ji ni okimasu ka.　　What time do you get up every morning?
　　…6-ji ni okimasu.　　　　　　…I get up at six.

4. N(time) *ni* V

　When a verb denotes a momentary action or movement, the time when it occurs is marked with the particle *ni*. *ni* is added when the noun before it uses a numeral. It can also be added to the days of the week, though it is not essential. When the noun does not use a numeral, *ni* is not added.

　⑨ 6-ji han ni okimasu.　　　　　I get up at six thirty.
　⑩ 7-gatsu futsuka ni Nihon e kimashita.　I came to Japan on July 2nd. (L. 5)
　⑪ Nichi-yōbi [ni] Nara e ikimasu.　I'm going to Nara on Sunday. (L. 5)
　⑫ Kinō benkyō-shimashita.　　　I studied yesterday.

5. N₁ *kara* N₂ *made*

1) *kara* indicates the starting time or place, and *made* indicates the finishing time or place.

　⑬ 9-ji kara 5-ji made hatarakimasu.　I work from nine to five.
　⑭ Ōsaka kara Tōkyō made 3-jikan kakarimasu.
　　　It takes three hours from Osaka to Tokyo. (L.11)

2) *kara* and *made* are not always used together.

　⑮ 9-ji kara hatarakimasu.　　　I work from nine.

3) ~*kara*, ~*made* or ~*kara* ~*made* is sometimes used with *desu* added directly after either.

　⑯ Ginkō wa 9-ji kara 3-ji made desu.　The bank is open from nine to three.
　⑰ Hiruyasumi wa 12-ji kara desu.　Lunchtime starts at twelve.

6. N₁ *to* N₂

　The particle *to* connects two nouns in coordinate relation.

　⑱ Ginkō no yasumi wa do-yōbi to nichi-yōbi desu.
　　　The bank is closed on Saturdays and Sundays.

7. S *ne*

　ne is attached to the end of a sentence to add feeling to what the speaker says. It shows the speaker's sympathy or the speaker's expectation that the listener will agree. In the latter usage, it is often used to confirm something.

　⑲ Mainichi 10-ji goro made benkyō-shimasu.
　　　…Taihen desu ne.
　　I study till about ten every day.
　　　…That must be hard.
　⑳ Yamada-san no denwa-bangō wa 871 no 6813 desu.
　　　…871 no 6813 desu ne.
　　Mr. Yamada's telephone number is 871-6813.
　　　…871-6813, right?

Lesson 5

I. Vocabulary

ikimasu	いきます	go
kimasu	きます	come
kaerimasu	かえります	go home, return
gakkō	がっこう	school
sūpā	スーパー	supermarket
eki	えき	station
hikōki	ひこうき	airplane
fune	ふね	ship
densha	でんしゃ	electric train
chikatetsu	ちかてつ	subway, underground
shinkansen	しんかんせん	the Shinkansen, the bullet train
basu	バス	bus
takushii	タクシー	taxi
jitensha	じてんしゃ	bicycle
aruite	あるいて	on foot
hito	ひと	person, people
tomodachi	ともだち	friend
kare	かれ	he, boyfriend, lover
kanojo	かのじょ	she, girlfriend, lover
kazoku	かぞく	family
hitori de	ひとりで	alone, by oneself
senshū	せんしゅう	last week
konshū	こんしゅう	this week
raishū	らいしゅう	next week
sengetsu	せんげつ	last month
kongetsu	こんげつ	this month
raigetsu	らいげつ	next month
kyonen	きょねん	last year
kotoshi	ことし	this year
rainen	らいねん	next year

－gatsu	－がつ	-th month of the year
nan-gatsu	なんがつ	what month
tsuitachi	ついたち	first day of the month
futsùka	ふつか	second, two days
mikka	みっか	third, three days
yokka	よっか	fourth, four days
itsuka	いつか	fifth, five days
muika	むいか	sixth, six days
nanoka	なのか	seventh, seven days
yōka	ようか	eighth, eight days
kokonoka	ここのか	ninth, nine days
tōka	とおか	tenth, ten days
jū-yokka	じゅうよっか	fourteenth, fourteen days
hatsuka	はつか	twentieth, twenty days
ni-jū-yokka	にじゅうよっか	twenty fourth, twenty four days
－nichi	－にち	-th day of the month, － days
nan-nichi	なんにち	which day of the month, how many days
itsu	いつ	when
tanjōbi	たんじょうび	birthday
futsū	ふつう	local (train)
kyūkō	きゅうこう	rapid
tokkyū	とっきゅう	express
tsugi no	つぎの	next

◁ Kaiwa ▷

Dō itashimashite.	どう いたしまして。	You're welcome./Don't mention it.
－bansen	－ばんせん	platform －, -th platform

〜〜〜〜〜〜〜〜〜〜〜〜〜〜〜〜〜〜〜〜〜〜

Hakata	はかた	name of a town in Kyushu
Fushimi	ふしみ	name of a town in Kyoto
Kōshien	こうしえん	name of a town near Osaka
Ōsakajō	おおさかじょう	Osaka Castle, a famous castle in Osaka

II. Translation

Sentence Patterns
1. I [will] go to Kyoto.
2. I [will] go home by taxi.
3. I came to Japan with my family.

Example Sentences
1. Where will you go tomorrow?
   ···I will go to Nara.
2. Where did you go last Sunday?
   ···I didn't go anywhere.
3. How will you go to Tokyo?
   ···I will go by Shinkansen.
4. Who will you go to Tokyo with?
   ···I will go with Mr. Yamada.
5. When did you come to Japan?
   ···I came here on March 25th.
6. When is your birthday?
   ···It is June 13th.

Conversation
Does this train go to Koshien?

Santos:	Excuse me. How much is it to Koshien?
Woman :	It's 350 yen.
Santos:	350 yen? Thank you very much.
Woman :	You're welcome.

Santos:	Excuse me. What platform is it for Koshien?
Station employee:	No. 5.
Santos:	Thanks.

Santos:	Excuse me. Does this train go to Koshien?
Man:	No, it doesn't. The next "local train" does.
Santos:	Thank you very much.

III. Reference Words & Information

SHUKUSAIJITSU   NATIONAL HOLIDAYS

1-gatsu tsuitachi	Ganjitsu	New Year's Day
1-gatsu dai-2 getsu-yōbi**	Seijin no hi	Coming-of-Age Day
2-gatsu 11-nichi	Kenkoku kinen no hi	National Foundation Day
3-gatsu hatsuka*	Shunbun no hi	Vernal Equinox Day
4-gatsu 29-nichi	Midori no hi	Greenery Day
5-gatsu mikka	Kenpō kinenbi	Constitution Memorial Day
5-gatsu yokka	Kokumin no kyūjitsu	Nation's Day
5-gatsu itsuka	Kodomo no hi	Children's Day
7-gatsu hatsuka	Umi no hi	Marine Day
9-gatsu 15-nichi	Keirō no hi	Respect-for-the-Aged Day
9-gatsu 23-nichi*	Shūbun no hi	Autumnal Equinox Day
10-gatsu dai-2 getsu-yōbi**	Taiiku no hi	Health and Sports Day
11-gatsu mikka	Bunka no hi	Culture Day
11-gatsu 23-nichi	Kinrō-kansha no hi	Labor Thanksgiving Day
12-gatsu 23-nichi	Tennō-tanjōbi	The Emperor's Birthday

* Varies from year to year.
** The second Monday

> If a national holiday falls on a Sunday, the following Monday is taken off instead. From April 29th to May 5th is a series of holidays, called **Gōruden-uiiku** (Golden Week). Some big companies give a whole week's holiday to employees.

IV. Grammar Explanation

1. **N(place) *e ikimasu/kimasu/kaerimasu***

   When a verb indicates movement to a certain place, the particle *e* is put after the place noun to show the direction of the move.

   ① Kyōto e ikimasu. 　　　　I will go to Kyoto.
   ② Nihon e kimashita. 　　　I came to Japan.
   ③ Uchi e kaerimasu. 　　　　I will go home.

2. **Doko [e] mo ikimasen/ikimasendeshita**

   When an interrogative takes the particle *mo* and the verb following it is negative, all that is represented by the interrogative is denied.

   ④ Doko [e] mo ikimasen. 　　I don't go anywhere.
   ⑤ Nani mo tabemasen. 　　　I don't eat anything. (L. 6)
   ⑥ Dare mo imasen. 　　　　　Nobody is there. (L. 10)

3. **N(vehicle) *de ikimasu/kimasu/kaerimasu***

   The particle *de* indicates a means or a method. When verbs denoting movement (*ikimasu, kimasu, kaerimasu*, etc.) are used with *de*, *de* indicates a means of transportation. The noun preceding *de* is a vehicle in this case.

   ⑦ Densha de ikimasu. 　　　I'll go by train.
   ⑧ Takushii de kimashita. 　　I came by taxi.

   When you walk somewhere, you use the expression *aruite*. In this case, *de* is not used.

   ⑨ Eki kara aruite kaerimashita. 　I walked home from the station.

4. **N(person/animal) *to* V**

   When you do something with a person (or an animal), the person (or the animal) is marked with the particle *to*.

   ⑩ Kazoku to Nihon e kimashita. 　I came to Japan with my family.

   If you do something alone, the expression *hitori de* is used. In this case, *to* is not used.

   ⑪ Hitori de Tōkyō e ikimasu. 　　I'll go to Tokyo alone.

5. *itsu*

To ask about time, the interrogatives using *nan* such as *nan-ji*, *nan-yōbi* and *nan-gatsu nan-nichi* are used. Other than these, the interrogative *itsu* (when) is also used to ask when something will happen/happened. *itsu* does not take the particle *ni*.

⑫ Itsu Nihon e kimashita ka.　　　　　　When did you come to Japan?
　　···3-gatsu 25-nichi ni kimashita.　　　···I came on March 25th.

⑬ Itsu Hiroshima e ikimasu ka.　　　　　When will you go to Hiroshima?
　　···Raishū ikimasu.　　　　　　　　　···I'll go there next week.

6. S *yo*

yo is placed at the end of a sentence. It is used to emphasize information which the listener does not know, or to show that you are giving your judgement or views assertively.

⑭ Kono densha wa Kōshien e ikimasu ka.
　　···Iie, ikimasen. Tsugi no futsū desu yo.
　　Does this train go to Koshien?
　　···No, it doesn't. The next local train does.

⑮ Murina daietto wa karada ni yokunai desu yo.
　　Excessive dieting is bad for your health. (L. 19)

Lesson 6

I. Vocabulary

tabemasu	たべます	eat
nomimasu	のみます	drink
suimasu	すいます	smoke [a cigarette]
[tabako o ~]	[たばこを ~]	
mimasu	みます	see, look at, watch
kikimasu	ききます	hear, listen
yomimasu	よみます	read
kakimasu	かきます	write, draw, paint
kaimasu	かいます	buy
torimasu	とります	take [a photograph]
[shashin o ~]	[しゃしんを ~]	
shimasu	します	do
aimasu	あいます	meet [a friend]
[tomodachi ni ~]	[ともだちに ~]	
gohan	ごはん	a meal, cooked rice
asagohan	あさごはん	breakfast
hirugohan	ひるごはん	lunch
bangohan	ばんごはん	supper
pan	パン	bread
tamago	たまご	egg
niku	にく	meat
sakana	さかな	fish
yasai	やさい	vegetable
kudamono	くだもの	fruit
mizu	みず	water
ocha	おちゃ	tea, green tea
kōcha	こうちゃ	black tea
gyūnyū	ぎゅうにゅう	milk
(miruku)	(ミルク)	
jūsu	ジュース	juice
biiru	ビール	beer
[o-]sake	[お]さけ	alcohol, Japanese rice wine

bideo	ビデオ	video tape, video deck
eiga	えいが	movie
CD	ＣＤ	CD, compact disc
tegami	てがみ	letter
repōto	レポート	report
shashin	しゃしん	photograph
mise	みせ	store, shop
resutoran	レストラン	restaurant
niwa	にわ	garden
shukudai	しゅくだい	homework (〜*o shimasu* : do homework)
tenisu	テニス	tennis (〜*o shimasu* : play tennis)
sakkā	サッカー	soccer, football (〜*o shimasu* : play soccer)
[o-]hanami	[お]はなみ	cherry-blossom viewing (〜*o shimasu* : go cherry-blossom viewing)
nani	なに	what
issho ni	いっしょに	together
chotto	ちょっと	a little while, a little bit
itsumo	いつも	always, usually
tokidoki	ときどき	sometimes
sorekara	それから	after that, and then
ē	ええ	yes
Ii desu ne.	いいですね。	That's good.
Wakarimashita.	わかりました。	I see.

◀ Kaiwa ▶

Nan desu ka.	なんですか。	Yes?
Ja mata [ashita].	じゃ、また［あした］。	See you [tomorrow].

Mekishiko	メキシコ	Mexico
Ōsakajō-kōen	おおさかじょうこうえん	Osaka Castle park

II. Translation

Sentence Patterns
1. I drink juice.
2. I buy a newspaper at the station.
3. Won't you come to Kobe with me?
4. Let's take a rest for a little bit.

Example Sentences
1. Do you smoke?
   ⋯No, I don't.
2. What do you eat every morning?
   ⋯I have egg and toast.
3. What did you eat this morning?
   ⋯I didn't eat anything.
4. What did you do last Saturday?
   ⋯I studied Japanese. Then I saw a movie.
   On Sunday what did you do?
   ⋯I went to Nara with a friend.
5. Where did you buy that bag?
   ⋯I bought it in Mexico.
6. Won't you drink some beer with me?
   ⋯Yes, let's have a drink.

Conversation
Won't you join us?

Sato:	Mr. Miller.
Miller:	Yes?
Sato:	I'm going to enjoy cherry-blossom viewing with my friends tomorrow. Won't you join us, Mr. Miller?
Miller:	That sounds nice. Where will you go?
Sato:	Osakajo-Koen.
Miller:	What time?
Sato:	At ten o'clock. Let's meet at Osakajo-Koen Station.
Miller:	OK.
Sato:	Well, see you tomorrow.

III. Reference Words & Information

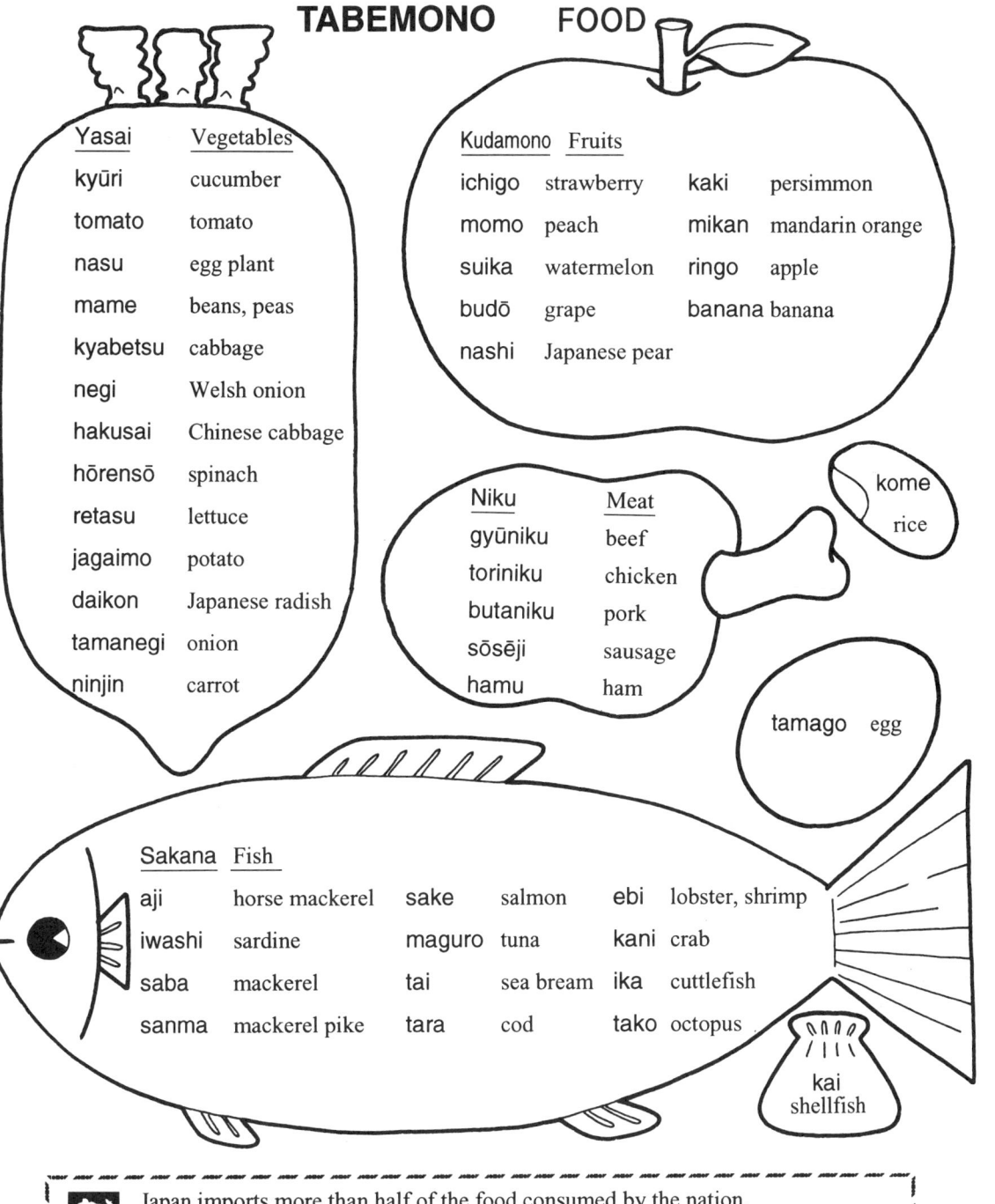

TABEMONO   FOOD

Yasai — Vegetables
- kyūri — cucumber
- tomato — tomato
- nasu — egg plant
- mame — beans, peas
- kyabetsu — cabbage
- negi — Welsh onion
- hakusai — Chinese cabbage
- hōrensō — spinach
- retasu — lettuce
- jagaimo — potato
- daikon — Japanese radish
- tamanegi — onion
- ninjin — carrot

Kudamono — Fruits
- ichigo — strawberry
- momo — peach
- suika — watermelon
- budō — grape
- nashi — Japanese pear
- kaki — persimmon
- mikan — mandarin orange
- ringo — apple
- banana — banana

Niku — Meat
- gyūniku — beef
- toriniku — chicken
- butaniku — pork
- sōsēji — sausage
- hamu — ham

kome — rice

tamago — egg

Sakana — Fish
- aji — horse mackerel
- iwashi — sardine
- saba — mackerel
- sanma — mackerel pike
- sake — salmon
- maguro — tuna
- tai — sea bream
- tara — cod
- ebi — lobster, shrimp
- kani — crab
- ika — cuttlefish
- tako — octopus

kai — shellfish

Japan imports more than half of the food consumed by the nation. The rates of self supply of food are as follows: cereals 29%, vegetables 86%, fruits 47%, meat 55%, and sea food 70% (1996, Ministry of Agriculture, Forestry, & Fisheries). Of all the cereals, rice is the only one that Japan is self-sufficient in.

IV. Grammar Explanation

1. **N o V(transitive)**

   o is used to indicate the direct object of a transitive verb.

   ① Jūsu o nomimasu.   I drink juice.

2. **N o shimasu**

   The words used as the objects of the verb *shimasu* cover a fairly wide range. *shimasu* means that the action denoted by the noun is performed. Some examples are shown below.

   1) to "play" sports or games

       sakkā o shimasu   play football
       toranpu o shimasu   play cards

   2) to "hold" gatherings

       pātii o shimasu   give a party
       kaigi o shimasu   hold a meeting

   3) to "do" something

       shukudai o shimasu   do homework
       shigoto o shimasu   do one's work

3. *Nani o shimasu ka*

   This is a question to ask what someone does.

   ② Getsu-yōbi nani o shimasu ka.   What will you do on Monday?
      ···Kyōto e ikimasu.   ···I'll go to Kyoto.
   ③ Kinō nani o shimashita ka.   What did you do yesterday?
      ···Sakkā o shimashita.   ···I played football.

   [Note] You can make a word expressing time the topic by adding *wa*.

   ④ Getsu-yōbi wa nani o shimasu ka. On Monday what will you do?
      ···Kyōto e ikimasu.   ···I'll go to Kyoto.

4. *nan* and *nani*

   Both *nan* and *nani* mean "what."

   1) *nan* is used in the following cases.

   (1) When it precedes a word whose first mora is either in the *t*, *d* or *n*-row.

   ⑤ Sore wa nan <u>d</u>esu ka.   What is that?
   ⑥ Nan <u>n</u>o hon desu ka.   What is the book about?
   ⑦ Neru mae ni, nan <u>t</u>o iimasu ka.
      What do you say before going to bed? (L. 21)

(2) When it is followed by a counter suffix or the like.

⑧ Teresa-chan wa nan-sai desu ka.　　How old is Teresa?

2) *nani* is used in all other cases.

⑨ Nani o kaimasu ka.　　What will you buy?

5. N (place) *de* V

When added after a noun denoting a place, *de* indicates the place where an action occurs.

⑩ Eki de shinbun o kaimasu.　　I buy the newspaper at the station.

6. V-*masen ka*

When you want to invite someone to do something, this expression is used.

⑪ Issho ni Kyōto e ikimasen ka.
　…Ē, ii desu ne.
Won't you come to Kyoto with us?
　…That's a nice idea.

7. V-*mashō*

This expression is used when a speaker is positively inviting the listener to do something with the speaker. It is also used when responding positively to an invitation.

⑫ Chotto yasumimashō.　　Let's have a break.

⑬ Issho ni hirugohan o tabemasen ka.
　…Ē, tabemashō.
Won't you have lunch with me?
　…Yes, let's go and eat.

[Note] An invitation using V-*masen ka* shows more consideration to the listener's will than that using V-*mashō*.

8. *o*～

You learned in Lesson 3 that the prefix *o* is attached to words regarding the listener or the person being referred to to show respect (e.g., [*o-*]*kuni* country).

o is also attached to various other words when the speaker is speaking politely (e.g., [*o-*]*sake* alcohol, [*o-*]*hanami* cherry-blossom viewing).

There are some words that are usually used with *o* without meaning respect or politeness (e.g., *ocha* tea, *okane* money).

Lesson 7

I. Vocabulary

kirimasu	きります	cut, slice
okurimasu	おくります	send
agemasu	あげます	give
moraimasu	もらいます	receive
kashimasu	かします	lend
karimasu	かります	borrow
oshiemasu	おしえます	teach
naraimasu	ならいます	learn
kakemasu	かけます	make [a telephone call]
[denwa o ~]	[でんわを ~]	
te	て	hand, arm
hashi	はし	chopsticks
supūn	スプーン	spoon
naifu	ナイフ	knife
fōku	フォーク	fork
hasami	はさみ	scissors
fakusu	ファクス	fax
wāpuro	ワープロ	word processor
pasokon	パソコン	personal computer
panchi	パンチ	punch
hotchikisu	ホッチキス	stapler
serotēpu	セロテープ	Scotch tape, clear adhesive tape
keshigomu	けしゴム	eraser
kami	かみ	paper
hana	はな	flower, blossom
shatsu	シャツ	shirt
purezento	プレゼント	present, gift
nimotsu	にもつ	baggage, parcel
okane	おかね	money
kippu	きっぷ	ticket
Kurisumasu	クリスマス	Christmas

chichi	ちち	(my) father
haha	はは	(my) mother
otōsan	おとうさん	(someone else's) father
okāsan	おかあさん	(someone else's) mother
mō	もう	already
mada	まだ	not yet
korekara	これから	from now on, soon
[〜,] suteki desu ne.	[〜、]すてきですね。	What a nice [〜]!

◁ Kaiwa ▷

Gomenkudasai.	ごめんください。	Excuse me./Anybody home?/May I come in? (an expression used by a visitor)
Irasshai.	いらっしゃい。	How nice of you to come. (lit. Welcome.)
Dōzo oagari kudasai.	どうぞ おあがり ください。	Do come in.
Shitsurei-shimasu.	しつれいします。	Thank you./May I? (lit. I'm afraid I'll be disturbing you.)
[〜 wa] ikaga desu ka.	[〜は]いかがですか。	Won't you have [〜]?/Would you like to have [〜]? (used when offering something)
Itadakimasu.	いただきます。	Thank you./I accept. (said before starting to eat or drink)
ryokō	りょこう	trip, tour (〜 o shimasu : travel, make a trip)
omiyage	おみやげ	souvenir, present

〜〜〜〜〜〜〜〜〜〜〜〜〜〜〜〜〜〜〜〜

Yōroppa	ヨーロッパ	Europe
Supein	スペイン	Spain

II. Translation

Sentence Patterns

1. I write letters with a word processor.
2. I [will] give some flowers to Ms. Kimura.
3. I received some chocolates from Ms. Karina.

Example Sentences

1. Did you study Japanese through television?
   ···No, I studied it through radio.
2. Do you write reports in Japanese?
   ···No. I write them in English.
3. What is "Good-bye" in Japanese?
   ···It is "Sayonara."
4. Who will you write Christmas cards to?
   ···To my family and friends.
5. What is that?
   ···It's a pocket notebook. I received it from Mr. Yamada.
6. Have you bought your Shinkansen ticket?
   ···Yes, I have.
7. Have you finished lunch?
   ···No, not yet. I am going to eat now.

Conversation

Hello

Jose Santos:	Hello.
Yamada Ichiro:	Hello. Please come in.
Jose Santos:	Thank you.
Yamada Tomoko:	How about a cup of coffee?
Maria Santos:	Thank you.
Yamada Tomoko:	Here you are.
Maria Santos:	Thank you.
	This spoon is nice, isn't it?
Yamada Tomoko:	Yes, it is. Someone in my company gave it to me.
	It's a souvenir of her trip to Europe.

III. Reference Words & Information

KAZOKU   FAMILY

WATASHI NO KAZOKU   MY FAMILY

- sobo — grandmother
- sofu — grandfather
- sofubo — grandparents
- haha — mother
- chichi — father
- ryōshin — parents
- imōto — younger sister
- otōto — younger brother
- ane — elder sister
- ani — elder brother
- kyōdai — brothers & sisters
- tsuma — wife
- (otto — husband)
- fūfu — husband & wife
- watashi — I
- musume — daughter
- musuko — son
- kodomo — children

TANAKA-SAN NO KAZOKU   Mr. (Ms.) TANAKA'S FAMILY

- obāsan — grandmother
- ojiisan — grandfather
- okāsan — mother
- otōsan — father
- go-ryōshin — parents
- imōto-san — younger sister
- otōto-san — younger brother
- onēsan — elder sister
- oniisan — elder brother
- go-kyōdai — brothers & sisters
- okusan — wife
- (go-shujin — husband)
- go-fūfu — husband & wife
- Tanaka-san — Mr. TANAKA (Ms. TANAKA)
- musume-san — daughter
- musuko-san — son
- okosan — children

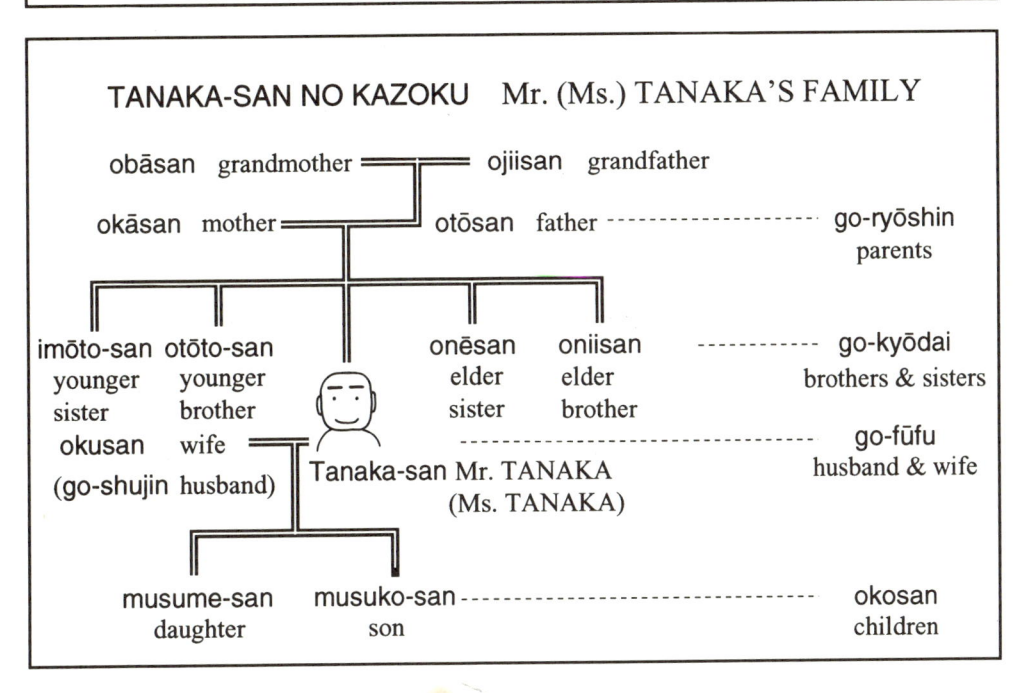

IV. Grammar Explanation

1. N (tool/means) *de* V

   The particle *de* indicates a method or a mean used for an action.

   ① Hashi de tabemasu.　　　　　　I eat with chopsticks.

   ② Nihon-go de repōto o kakimasu.　　I write a report in Japanese.

2. "Word/Sentence" *wa* ~*go de nan desu ka*

   This question is used to ask how to say a word or a sentence in other languages.

   ③ "Arigatō" wa Eigo de nan desu ka.
   　…"Thank you" desu.
   　What's "arigatō" in English?
   　… It's "Thank you."

   ④ "Thank you" wa Nihon-go de nan desu ka.
   　…"Arigatō" desu.
   　What's "Thank you" in Japanese?
   　… It's "arigatō."

3. N (person) *ni agemasu*, etc.

   Verbs like *agemasu, kashimasu, oshiemasu*, etc., need persons to whom you give, lend, teach, etc. The persons are marked with *ni*.

   ⑤ Yamada-san wa Kimura-san ni hana o agemashita.
   　Mr. Yamada gave flowers to Ms. Kimura.

   ⑥ Ii-san ni hon o kashimashita.
   　I lent my book to Ms. Lee.

   ⑦ Tarō-kun ni Eigo o oshiemasu.
   　I teach Taro English.

   [Note] With verbs like *okurimasu, denwa o kakemasu*, etc., place nouns can be used instead of N(person). In this case, the particle *e* is sometimes used instead of *ni*.

   ⑧ Kaisha ni denwa o kakemasu.
   　　　　(e)
   　I'll call my office.

4. N (person) *ni moraimasu*, etc.

Verbs like *moraimasu*, *karimasu* and *naraimasu* express actions from the receiving side. The persons from whom you receive those actions are marked with *ni*.

⑨ Kimura-san wa Yamada-san ni hana o moraimashita.
　　Ms. Kimura received flowers from Mr. Yamada.

⑩ Karina-san ni CD o karimashita.
　　I borrowed a CD from Ms. Karina.

⑪ Wan-san ni Chūgoku-go o naraimasu.
　　I learn Chinese from Mr. Wang.

kara is sometimes used instead of *ni* in this sentence pattern. When you receive something from an organization like a school or a company, only *kara* is used.

⑫ Kimura-san wa Yamada-san kara hana o moraimashita.
　　Ms. Kimura received flowers from Mr. Yamada.

⑬ Ginkō kara okane o karimashita.
　　I borrowed some money from the bank.

5. *Mō* V-*mashita*

mō means "already" and is used with V-*mashita*. In this case, V-*mashita* means that the action has been finished.
　The answer to the question *mō* V-*mashita ka* is *hai, mō* V-*mashita* or *iie, mada desu*.

⑭ Mō nimotsu o okurimashita ka.　　　Have you sent the parcel yet?
　　···Hai, [mō] okurimashita.　　　　　···Yes, I have [already sent it].
　　···Iie, mada desu.　　　　　　　　　···No, not yet.

In giving a negative answer to this type of question, you should not use V-*masendeshita*, as this simply means you did not do the specified task rather than you have not done it yet.

Lesson 8

I. Vocabulary

hansamu[na]	ハンサム[な]	handsome
kirei[na]	きれい[な]	beautiful, clean
shizuka[na]	しずか[な]	quiet
nigiyaka[na]	にぎやか[な]	lively
yūmei[na]	ゆうめい[な]	famous
shinsetsu[na]	しんせつ[な]	kind
genki[na]	げんき[な]	healthy, sound, cheerful
hima[na]	ひま[な]	free (time)
benri[na]	べんり[な]	convenient
suteki[na]	すてき[な]	fine, nice, wonderful
ōkii	おおきい	big, large
chiisai	ちいさい	small, little
atarashii	あたらしい	new
furui	ふるい	old (not of age)
ii (yoi)	いい (よい)	good
warui	わるい	bad
atsui	あつい	hot
samui	さむい	cold (referring to temperature)
tsumetai	つめたい	cold (referring to touch)
muzukashii	むずかしい	difficult
yasashii	やさしい	easy
takai	たかい	expensive, tall, high
yasui	やすい	inexpensive
hikui	ひくい	low
omoshiroi	おもしろい	interesting
oishii	おいしい	delicious, tasty
isogashii	いそがしい	busy
tanoshii	たのしい	enjoyable
shiroi	しろい	white
kuroi	くろい	black
akai	あかい	red
aoi	あおい	blue
sakura	さくら	cherry (blossom)
yama	やま	mountain

machi	まち	town, city
tabemono	たべもの	food
kuruma	くるま	car, vehicle
tokoro	ところ	place
ryō	りょう	dormitory
benkyō	べんきょう	study
seikatsu	せいかつ	life
[o-]shigoto	[お]しごと	work, business (~o shimasu : do one's job, work)
dō	どう	how
donna ~	どんな～	what kind of ~
dore	どれ	which one (of three or more)
totemo	とても	very
amari	あまり	not so (used with negatives)
soshite	そして	and (used to connect sentences)
~ ga, ~	～が、～	~, but ~
O-genki desu ka.	おげんきですか。	How are you?
Sō desu ne.	そうですね。	Well let me see. (pausing)

◁ Kaiwa ▷

Nihon no seikatsu ni naremashita ka.	にほんの せいかつに なれましたか。	Have you got used to the life in Japan?
[~,] mō ippai ikaga desu ka.	[～、]もう いっぱい いかがですか。	Won't you have another cup of [~]?
Iie, kekkō desu.	いいえ、けっこうです。	No, thank you.
Mō ~ desu [ne].	もう ～です[ね]。	It's already ~[, isn't it?].
Sorosoro shitsurei-shimasu.	そろそろ しつれいします。	It's almost time to leave now.
Mata irasshatte kudasai.	また いらっしゃって ください。	Please come again.

〜〜〜〜〜〜〜〜〜〜〜〜〜〜〜〜〜〜

Fujisan	ふじさん	Mt. Fuji, the highest mountain in Japan
Biwako	びわこ	Lake Biwa, the biggest lake in Japan
Shanhai	シャンハイ	Shanghai
"Shichi-nin no Samurai"	「しちにんの さむらい」	"The Seven Samurai," a classic movie by Akira Kurosawa
Kinkakuji	きんかくじ	Kinkakuji Temple (the Golden Pavilion)

II. Translation

Sentence Patterns

1. Cherry blossoms are beautiful.
2. Mt. Fuji is high.
3. Cherry blossoms are beautiful flowers.
4. Mt. Fuji is a high mountain.

Example Sentences

1. Is Osaka lively?
   ⋯Yes, it is.
2. Is the water of Lake Biwa clean?
   ⋯No, it is not so clean.
3. Is it cold in Beijing now?
   ⋯Yes, it is very cold.
   Is it cold in Shanghai, too?
   ⋯No, it is not so cold.
4. Is that dictionary good?
   ⋯No, it is not so good.
5. How do you like the subway in Tokyo?
   ⋯It is clean. And it is convenient.
6. I saw a movie yesterday.
   ⋯What kind of movie was it?
   It was "The Seven Samurai." It is old, but a very interesting movie.
7. Which is Mr. Miller's umbrella?
   ⋯That blue one is.

Conversation

It's almost time to leave

Yamada Ichiro:	Have you got accustomed to living in Japan, Maria?
Maria Santos:	Yes, I have. I enjoy it every day.
Yamada Ichiro:	Really? Mr. Santos, how is your work?
Jose Santos:	Well, it's busy, but interesting.

Yamada Tomoko:	Would you like another cup of coffee?
Maria Santos:	No, thank you.

Jose Santos:	Oh, it's eight o'clock now. We must be going.
Yamada Ichiro:	You must?
Maria Santos:	Thank you for everything today.
Yamada Tomoko:	Our pleasure. Please come again.

III. Reference Words & Information

IRO · AJI   COLOR & TASTE

Iro Color

noun	adjective	noun	adjective
shiro white	shiroi	kiiro yellow	kiiroi
kuro black	kuroi	chairo brown	chairoi
aka red	akai	pinku pink	—
ao blue	aoi	orenji orange	—
midori green	—	gurē gray	—
murasaki purple	—	bēju beige	—

Aji Taste

amai sweet   karai hot    nigai bitter    shiokarai salty

suppai sour    koi thick, strong    usui thin, weak

Haru · Natsu · Aki · Fuyu Spring·Summer·Autumn·Winter

There are four seasons in Japan, spring (March, April, May), summer (June, July, August), autumn (September, October, November), and winter (December, January, February). The average temperature varies from place to place, but the change patterns are almost the same (see the graph).

The hottest month is August and the coldest, January or February. So Japanese people feel that "summer is hot," "autumn is cool," "winter is cold," and "spring is warm."

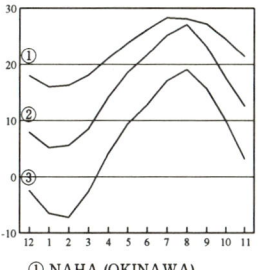

① NAHA (OKINAWA)
② TOKYO
③ ABASHIRI (HOKKAIDO)

IV. Grammar Explanation

1. Adjectives

   Adjectives are used as 1) predicates and 2) noun modifiers. They inflect and are divided into two groups, *i*-adjectives and *na*-adjectives, according to the inflection.

2.
   > N *wa na*-adj *[ná] desu*
   > N *wa i*-adj *(~i) desu*

   1) *desu* at the end of an adjective sentence shows the speaker's polite attitude toward the listener. An *i*-adjective with *i* at the end comes before *desu*, whereas a *na*-adjective without *[na]* comes before *desu*.

      ① Watto-sensei wa shinsetsu desu.   Mr. Watt is kind.
      ② Fujisan wa takai desu.   Mt. Fuji is high.

      desu is used when a sentence is non-past and affirmative.

   2) *na*-adj *[ná] ja arimasen*
      The negative form of *na*-adj *[ná] desu* is *na*-adj *[ná] ja arimasen*.
      (*na*-adj *[ná] dewa arimasen*)

      ③ Asoko wa shizuka ja arimasen.   It's not quiet there.
                         (dewa)

   3) *i*-adj *(~i) desu* → *~kunai desu*
      To make the negative form of an *i*- adjective, *i* at the end of the *i*-adjective is altered to *kunai*.

      ④ Kono hon wa omoshirokunai desu.   This book is not interesting.

      The negative for *ii desu* is *yokunai desu*.

   4) Questions using adjective sentences are made in the same way as those using noun or verb sentences. In answering a question, you repeat the adjective used in the question. *sō desu* or *sō ja arimasen* cannot be used.

      ⑤ Pekin wa samui desu ka.   Is it cold in Beijing?
        ···Hai, samui desu.   ···Yes, it is.
      ⑥ Biwako no mizu wa kirei desu ka.   Is the water of Lake Biwa clean?
        ···Iie, kirei ja arimasen.   ···No, it isn't.

3.
   > *na*-adj *na* N
   > *i*-adj *(~i)* N

   An adjective is put before a noun to modify it. A *na*-adjective needs *na* before a noun.

      ⑦ Watto-sensei wa shinsetsuna sensei desu. Mr. Watt is a kind teacher.
      ⑧ Fujisan wa takai yama desu.   Mt. Fuji is a high mountain.

4. totemo/amari

totemo and *amari* are adverbs of degree. Both come before the adjectives they are modifying.
  totemo is used in affirmative sentences, and means "very." *amari* is used in negative sentences. *amari* and a negative form mean "not very."

⑨ Pekin wa totemo samui desu.
  Beijing is very cold.

⑩ Kore wa totemo yūmeina eiga desu.
  This is a very famous movie.

⑪ Shanhai wa amari samukunai desu.
  Shanghai is not very cold.

⑫ Sakura-daigaku wa amari yūmeina daigaku ja arimasen.
  Sakura University is not a very famous university.

5. N wa dō desu ka

This question is used to ask an impression or an opinion about a thing, place or person, etc., that the listener has experienced, visited or met.

⑬ Nihon no seikatsu wa dō desu ka. How is the life in Japan?
  ···Tanoshii desu.   ···It's enjoyable.

6. N₁ wa donna N₂ desu ka

When the speaker wants the listener to describe or explain N₁, this question pattern is used. N₂ denotes the category N₁ belongs to. The interrogative *donna* is always followed by a noun.

⑭ Nara wa donna machi desu ka. What kind of town is Nara?
  ···Furui machi desu.   ···It's an old town.

7. S₁ ga, S₂

ga is a conjunctive particle, meaning "but." It is used to link sentences.

⑮ Nihon no tabemono wa oishii desu ga, takai desu.
  Japanese food is good, but expensive.

8. dore

This interrogative is used to ask the listener to choose or designate one from more than two things concretely shown or named.

⑯ Mirā-san no kasa wa dore desu ka. Which is Mr. Miller's umbrella?
  ···Ano aoi kasa desu.   ···That blue one is.

Lesson 9

I. Vocabulary

wakarimasu	わかります	understand
arimasu	あります	have
suki[na]	すき[な]	like
kirai[na]	きらい[な]	dislike
jōzu[na]	じょうず[な]	good at
heta[na]	へた[な]	poor at
ryōri	りょうり	dish (cooked food), cooking
nomimono	のみもの	drinks
supōtsu	スポーツ	sport (~*o shimasu* : play sports)
yakyū	やきゅう	baseball (~*o shimasu* : play baseball)
dansu	ダンス	dance (~*o shimasu* : dance)
ongaku	おんがく	music
uta	うた	song
kurashikku	クラシック	classical music
jazu	ジャズ	jazz
konsāto	コンサート	concert
karaoke	カラオケ	karaoke
kabuki	かぶき	Kabuki (traditional Japanese musical drama)
e	え	picture, drawing
ji	じ	letter, character
kanji	かんじ	Chinese characters
hiragana	ひらがな	Hiragana script
katakana	かたかな	Katakana script
rōmaji	ローマじ	the Roman alphabet
komakai okane	こまかい おかね	small change
chiketto	チケット	ticket
jikan	じかん	time
yōji	ようじ	something to do, errand
yakusoku	やくそく	appointment, promise

go-shujin	ごしゅじん	(someone else's) husband
otto/shujin	おっと／しゅじん	(my) husband
okusan	おくさん	(someone else's) wife
tsuma/kanai	つま／かない	(my) wife
kodomo	こども	child
yoku	よく	well, much
daitai	だいたい	mostly, roughly
takusan	たくさん	many, much
sukoshi	すこし	a little, a few
zenzen	ぜんぜん	not at all (used with negatives)
hayaku	はやく	early, quickly, fast
~ kara	～から	because ~
dōshite	どうして	why
Zannen desu [ne].	ざんねんです[ね]。	I'm sorry (to hear that)./That's a pity.
Sumimasen.	すみません。	I am sorry.

◁ Kaiwa ▷

moshi moshi	もしもし	hello (used on the phone)
ā	ああ	oh
Issho ni ikaga desu ka.	いっしょに いかがですか。	Won't you join me (us)?
[~ wa] chotto…….	[～は] ちょっと……。	[~] is a bit difficult. (an euphemism used when declining an invitation)
Dame desu ka.	だめですか。	So you cannot (come)?
Mata kondo onegai-shimasu.	また こんど おねがいします。	Please ask me again some other time. (used when refusing an invitation indirectly, considering someone's feelings)

Ozawa Seiji	おざわ せいじ	famous Japanese conductor (1935－)

II. Translation

Sentence Patterns
1. I like Italian cuisine.
2. I understand Japanese a little.
3. Today is my child's birthday, so I will go home early.

Example Sentences
1. Do you like alcohol?
   ···No, I don't.
2. What kind of sports do you like?
   ···I like soccer.
3. Is Ms. Karina good at drawing pictures?
   ···Yes, she is very good at it.
4. Do you understand Indonesian, Mr. Tanaka?
   ···No, I do not understand it at all.
5. Do you have any small change?
   ···No, I don't.
6. Do you read newspapers every morning?
   ···No, as I don't have the time, I don't.
7. Why did you go home early yesterday?
   ···Because I had something to do.

Conversation

That's too bad

Miller:	Hello. This is Miller.
Kimura:	It's you, Mr. Miller. Good evening. How are you?
Miller:	Fine. Thank you.
	Well, Ms. Kimura. How would you like to go to a concert by Seiji Ozawa?
Kimura:	That sounds nice. When will it be?
Miller:	It's on Friday night of next week.
Kimura:	Friday?
	Friday's a bit difficult.
Miller:	So you can't come?
Kimura:	I have arranged to meet a friend on Friday night.
Miller:	You have. I'm sorry to hear that.
Kimura:	I am, too. Please invite me again some other time.

III. Reference Words & Information

ONGAKU · SUPŌTSU   MUSIC, SPORTS & MOVIES

Ongaku Music

poppusu	pop
rokku	rock
jazu	jazz
raten	Latin American music
kurashikku	classical music
min'yō	folk music
enka	traditional Japanese popular songs
myūjikaru	musical
opera	opera

Eiga Film

SF	SF film
horā	horror film
anime	animated film
dokyumentarii	documentary film
ren'ai	romantic film
misuterii	mystery film
bungei	movie based on a classic work
sensō	war film
akushon	action film
kigeki	comedy film

Supōtsu Sports

sofutobōru	softball	yakyū	baseball
sakkā	soccer	takkyū/pinpon	ping-pong
ragubii	rugby football	sumō	sumo
barēbōru	volleyball	jūdō	judo
basukettobōru	basketball	kendō	Japanese fencing
tenisu	tennis	suiei	swimming
bōringu	bowling		
sukii	skiing		
sukēto	skating		

IV. Grammar Explanation

1. N *ga arimasu/wakarimasu*
   N *ga suki desu/kirai desu/jōzu desu/heta desu*

   The object of a transitive verb is marked with o. However, objects of the verbs *arimasu* and *wakarimasu* are marked with *ga*.

   Such adjectives as *suki desu, kirai desu, jōzu desu* and *heta desu* require objects, and these are marked with *ga*, too. The verbs and adjectives whose objects are marked with *ga* are those kinds that describe preference, ability, possession and the like.

   ① Watashi wa Itaria-ryōri ga suki desu.   I like Italian food.
   ② Watashi wa Nihon-go ga wakarimasu.   I understand Japanese.
   ③ Watashi wa kuruma ga arimasu.   I have a car.

2. *donna* N

   Other than the usage you learned in Lesson 8, *donna* is also used to ask the listener to name one from a group which the noun after *donna* denotes.

   ④ Donna supōtsu ga suki desu ka.   What sports do you like?
   ···Sakkā ga suki desu.   ···I like football.

3. *yoku/daitai/takusan/sukoshi/amari/zenzen*

   These adverbs are put before verbs when they modify them. The following is a summary of their usage.

degree	adverb + affirmative	adverb + negative
high ↕ low	yoku wakarimasu daitai wakarimasu sukoshi wakarimasu	amari wakarimasen zenzen wakarimasen

amount	adverb + affirmative	adverb + negative
large ↕ small	takusan arimasu sukoshi arimasu	amari arimasen zenzen arimasen

⑤ Eigo ga yoku wakarimasu.   I understand English very well.
⑥ Eigo ga sukoshi wakarimasu.   I understand English a little.
⑦ Eigo ga amari wakarimasen.   I don't understand English so well.
⑧ Okane ga takusan arimasu.   I have a lot of money.
⑨ Okane ga zenzen arimasen.   I don't have any money.

[Note] *sukoshi* and *zenzen* can also modify adjectives.

⑩ Koko wa sukoshi samui desu.   It's a little cold here.
⑪ Ano eiga wa zenzen omoshirokunai desu.
That movie is not interesting at all.

4. S_1 *kara*, S_2

kara connects two sentences together to denote a causal relationship. S_1 is the reason for S_2.

⑫ Jikan ga arimasen kara, shinbun o yomimasen.
Because I don't have time, I don't read the newspaper.

You can also state S_2 first and add the reason after it.

⑬ Maiasa shinbun o yomimasu ka.
···Iie, yomimasen. Jikan ga arimasen kara.
Do you read a newspaper every morning?
···No, I don't. Because I have no time.

5. *dōshite*

The interrogative *dōshite* is used to ask a reason. The answer needs *kara* at the end.

⑭ Dōshite asa shinbun o yomimasen ka.
···Jikan ga arimasen kara.
Why don't you read a newspaper in the morning?
···Because I don't have time.

The question *dōshite desu ka* is also used to ask the reason for what the other person has said.

⑮ Kyō wa hayaku kaerimasu.   I'll go home early today.
···Dōshite desu ka.   ···Why?
Kodomo no tanjōbi desu kara.   Because today's my child's birthday.

Lesson 10

I. Vocabulary

imasu	います	exist, be (referring to animate things)
arimasu	あります	exist, be (referring to inanimate things)
iroiro[na]	いろいろ[な]	various
otoko no hito	おとこの ひと	man
onna no hito	おんなの ひと	woman
otoko no ko	おとこの こ	boy
onna no ko	おんなの こ	girl
inu	いぬ	dog
neko	ねこ	cat
ki	き	tree, wood
mono	もの	thing
firumu	フィルム	film
denchi	でんち	battery
hako	はこ	box
suitchi	スイッチ	switch
reizōko	れいぞうこ	refrigerator
tēburu	テーブル	table
beddo	ベッド	bed
tana	たな	shelf
doa	ドア	door
mado	まど	window
posuto	ポスト	mailbox, postbox
biru	ビル	building
kōen	こうえん	park
kissaten	きっさてん	coffee shop
hon-ya	ほんや	bookstore
~ ya	~や	~ store
noriba	のりば	a fixed place to catch taxis, trains, etc.
ken	けん	prefecture

ue	うえ	on, above, over
shita	した	under, below, beneath
mae	まえ	front, before
ushiro	うしろ	back, behind
migi	みぎ	right [side]
hidari	ひだり	left [side]
naka	なか	in, inside
soto	そと	outside
tonari	となり	next, next door
chikaku	ちかく	near, vicinity
aida	あいだ	between, among
～ ya ～[nado]	～や ～[など]	～, ～, and so on
ichiban ～	いちばん ～	the most ～ (*ichiban ue* : the top)
－dan-me	－だんめ	the -th shelf (*dan* is the counter for shelves)

◀ Kaiwa ▶

[Dōmo] sumimasen.	[どうも] すみません。	Thank you.
chiri-sōsu	チリソース	chili sauce
oku	おく	the back
supaisu-kōnā	スパイス・コーナー	spice corner

Tōkyō Dizuniirando	とうきょうディズニーランド	Tokyo Disneyland
Yunyūya-sutoa	ユニューヤ・ストア	fictitious supermarket

II. Translation

Sentence Patterns
1. Ms. Sato is over there.
2. There is a photo on the desk.
3. My family is in New York.
4. Tokyo Disneyland is in Chiba Prefecture.

Example Sentences
1. You see that man over there. Who is that?
   ···He is Mr. Matsumoto of IMC.
2. Is there a telephone near here?
   ···Yes, it is over there.
3. Who is in the garden?
   ···Nobody is. There is a cat.
4. What is there in the box?
   ···There are old letters and photos and so on.
5. Where is Mr. Miller?
   ···He is in the meeting room.
6. Where is the post office?
   ···It is near the station. It is in front of the bank.

Conversation
Do you have chili sauce in this store?

Miller:	Excuse me. Where is Yunyu-ya Store?
Woman:	Yunyu-ya Store?
	You see that white building over there?
	The store is in that building.
Miller:	I see. Thank you.
Woman:	Not at all.
	--
Miller:	Excuse me, do you have chili sauce?
Shop assistant:	Yes.
	There is a spice corner on the right-hand side at the back.
	Chili sauce is on the second rack from the bottom.
Miller:	I see. Thanks.

III. Reference Words & Information

UCHI NO NAKA   INSIDE THE HOUSE

① genkan   entrance hall
② toire   toilet
③ furoba   bathroom
④ senmenjo   washroom
⑤ daidokoro   kitchen
⑥ shokudō   dining room
⑦ ima   living room
⑧ shinshitsu bedroom
⑨ rōka   hallway
⑩ beranda   balcony

How to Use a Japanese Bath

① Wash and rinse yourself in the tiled area before getting in the bath.

② Soap and shampoo should never be used in the bath. The bath is for soaking and relaxing.

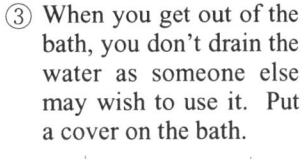

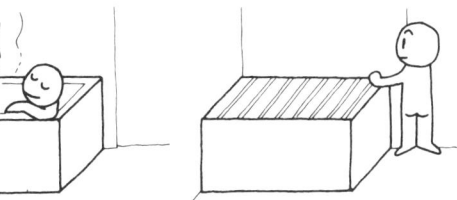

③ When you get out of the bath, you don't drain the water as someone else may wish to use it. Put a cover on the bath.

How to Use the Toilet

Japanese style   Western style

IV. Grammar Explanation

1. **N ga arimasu/imasu**

   This sentence pattern is used to indicate the existence or presence of a thing(s) or person(s). The thing(s) or person(s) in such a sentence is treated as the subject and marked with the particle *ga*.

   1) *arimasu* is used when what is present is inanimate or does not move by itself. Things, plants and places belong in this category.
      - ① Konpyūta ga arimasu.   There is a computer.
      - ② Sakura ga arimasu.   There are cherry trees.
      - ③ Kōen ga arimasu.   There is a park.

   2) When what is present is animate and moves by itself, *imasu* is used. People and animals belong in this category.
      - ④ Otoko no hito ga imasu.   There is a man.
      - ⑤ Inu ga imasu.   There is a dog.

2. **N₁ (place) ni N₂ ga arimasu/imasu**

   1) The place where N₂ is present is indicated by the particle *ni*.
      - ⑥ Watashi no heya ni tsukue ga arimasu.   There is a desk in my room.
      - ⑦ Jimusho ni Mirā-san ga imasu.   Mr. Miller is in the office.

   2) You can ask what or who is present at/in the place by using this pattern. The interrogative *nani* is used for things and *dare* is used for persons.
      - ⑧ Chika ni nani ga arimasu ka.   What is there in the basement?
           ⋯Resutoran ga arimasu.   ⋯There are restaurants.
      - ⑨ Uketsuke ni dare ga imasu ka.   Who is at the reception desk?
           ⋯Kimura-san ga imasu.   ⋯Ms. Kimura is there.

3. **N₁ wa N₂ (place) ni arimasu/imasu**

   1) In this sentence pattern, the speaker picks up N₁ as the topic, and explains where it is. The topic should be something or someone that both the speaker and the listener know about. The particle attached to N₁ is not *ga*, which marks the subject, but *wa*, which marks the topic.
      - ⑩ Tōkyō Dizuniirando wa Chiba-ken ni arimasu.
           Tokyo Disneyland is in Chiba Prefecture.
      - ⑪ Mirā-san wa jimusho ni imasu.   Mr. Miller is in the office.

   2) When you ask where N₁ is, this sentence pattern is used.
      - ⑫ Tōkyō Dizuniirando wa doko ni arimasu ka.
           ⋯Chiba-ken ni arimasu.
           Where is Tokyo Disneyland?
           ⋯It's in Chiba Prefecture.
      - ⑬ Mirā-san wa doko ni imasu ka.   Where is Mr. Miller?
           ⋯Jimusho ni imasu.   ⋯He's in the office.

[Note] *desu* is sometimes used to replace a verb predicate when the predicate is obvious. The sentence N₁ *wa* N₂(place) *ni arimasu/imasu* can be replaced by the sentence N₁ *wa* N₂(place) *desu*, which you learned in Lesson 3.

⑭ Tōkyō Dizuniirando wa doko ni arimasu ka.
　…Chiba-ken desu.
　Where is Tokyo Disneyland?
　…It's in Chiba Prefecture.

4. N₁(thing/person/place) *no* N₂(position)

ue, shita, mae, ushiro, migi, hidari, naka, soto, tonari, chikaku and *aida* are nouns denoting position.

⑮ Tsukue no ue ni shashin ga arimasu.　There is a picture on the desk.
⑯ Yūbinkyoku wa ginkō no tonari ni arimasu.　The post office is next to the bank.

[Note] As these are place nouns, not only *ni* but also particles like *de* can come after them.

⑰ Eki no chikaku de tomodachi ni aimashita.　I met a friend near the station.

5. N₁ *ya* N₂

Nouns are connected in coordinate relation by the particle *ya*. While *to* enumerates all the items, *ya* shows a few representative items. Sometimes *nado* is put after the last noun to explicitly express that there are also some other things of the kind.

⑱ Hako no naka ni tegami ya shashin ga arimasu.
　There are letters, pictures and so on in the box.
⑲ Hako no naka ni tegami ya shashin nado ga arimasu.
　There are letters, pictures and so on in the box.

6. Word(s) *desu ka*

The particle *ka* has the function to confirm. The speaker picks up a word or words he/she wants to confirm and confirms it (them) using this pattern.

⑳ Sumimasen. Yunyūya-sutoa wa doko desu ka.
　…Yunyūya-sutoa desu ka. Ano biru no naka desu.
　Excuse me, but where is Yunyu-ya Store?
　…Yunyu-ya Store? It's in that building.

7. *Chiri-sōsu wa arimasen ka*

The expression *chiri-sōsu wa arimasen ka* is found in the conversation of this lesson. By using the negative form *arimasen ka* instead of *arimasu ka*, you can be indirect and polite, showing that you are prepared for a negative answer.

Lesson 11

I. Vocabulary

imasu	います	have [a child]
[kodomo ga ~]	[こどもが~]	
imasu	います	stay, be [in Japan]
[Nihon ni ~]	[にほんに~]	
kakarimasu	かかります	take (referring to time or money)
yasumimasu	やすみます	take a day off [work]
[kaisha o ~]	[かいしゃを~]	
hitotsu	ひとつ	one (used when counting things)
futatsu	ふたつ	two
mittsu	みっつ	three
yottsu	よっつ	four
itsutsu	いつつ	five
muttsu	むっつ	six
nanatsu	ななつ	seven
yattsu	やっつ	eight
kokonotsu	ここのつ	nine
tō	とお	ten
ikutsu	いくつ	how many
hitori	ひとり	one person
futari	ふたり	two persons
－nin	－にん	－ people
－dai	－だい	(counter for machines, cars, etc.)
－mai	－まい	(counter for paper, stamps, etc.)
－kai	－かい	－ times
ringo	りんご	apple
mikan	みかん	mandarin orange
sandoitchi	サンドイッチ	sandwich
karē[-raisu]	カレー[ライス]	curry [and rice]
aisukuriimu	アイスクリーム	ice cream
kitte	きって	postage stamp
hagaki	はがき	post card
fūtō	ふうとう	envelope
sokutatsu	そくたつ	special delivery
kakitome	かきとめ	registered mail

eamēru (kōkūbin)	エアメール（こうくうびん）	airmail
funabin	ふなびん	sea mail
ryōshin	りょうしん	parents
kyōdai	きょうだい	brothers and sisters
ani	あに	(my) elder brother
oniisan	おにいさん	(someone else's) elder brother
ane	あね	(my) elder sister
onēsan	おねえさん	(someone else's) elder sister
otōto	おとうと	(my) younger brother
otōto-san	おとうとさん	(someone else's) younger brother
imōto	いもうと	(my) younger sister
imōto-san	いもうとさん	(someone else's) younger sister
gaikoku	がいこく	foreign country
－jikan	－じかん	－ hours
－shūkan	－しゅうかん	－ weeks
－kagetsu	－かげつ	－ months
－nen	－ねん	－ years
～gurai	～ぐらい	about ～
donokurai	どのくらい	how long
zenbu de	ぜんぶで	in total
minna	みんな	all, everything
～dake	～だけ	only ～
Irasshaimase.	いらっしゃいませ。	Welcome./May I help you? (a greeting to a customer or a guest entering a shop, etc.)

◀ Kaiwa ▶

Ii [o-]tenki desu ne.	いい[お]てんきですね。	Nice weather, isn't it?
O-dekake desu ka.	おでかけですか。	Are you going out?
Chotto ～ made.	ちょっと ～まで。	I'm just going to ～.
Itte irasshai.	いって いらっしゃい。	So long. (lit. Go and come back.)
Itte mairimasu.	いって まいります。	So long. (lit. I'm going and coming back.)
sorekara	それから	and, furthermore

Ōsutoraria	オーストラリア	Australia

II. Translation

Sentence Patterns
1. There are seven tables in the meeting room.
2. I will stay in Japan for one year.

Example Sentences
1. How many apples did you buy?
   ···I bought four.
2. Give me five 80-yen stamps and two postcards, please.
   ···Certainly. That's 500 yen in all.
3. Are there foreign teachers at Fuji University?
   ···Yes, there are three. They are all Americans.
4. How many people are there in your family?
   ···There are five. My parents, my elder sister, my elder brother and me.
5. How many times a week do you play tennis?
   ···I play it about twice a week.
6. How long did you study Spanish, Mr. Tanaka?
   ···I studied it for three months.
   Only three months? You speak it very well.
7. How long does it take from Osaka to Tokyo by Shinkansen?
   ···It takes two and a half hours.

Conversation
Please send this by sea mail

Janitor:	Nice weather, isn't it? Are you going out?
Wang:	Yes, I am going to the post office.
Janitor:	Really? See you later.
Wang:	See you.

Wang:	I would like to send this by special delivery.
Post office clerk:	Sure. To Australia? That's 370 yen.
Wang:	And also this parcel.
Post office clerk:	By sea mail or airmail?
Wang:	How much is sea mail?
Post office clerk:	500 yen.
Wang:	How long will it take?
Post office clerk:	It will take about one month.
Wang:	Well, please send it by sea mail.

III. Reference Words & Information

MENYŪ MENU

teishoku	set meal		
ranchi	set meal in the western style		
tendon	a bowl of rice with fried fish and vegetables	karē-raisu	curry and rice
oyakodon	a bowl of rice with chicken and egg	hanbāgu	hamburg steak
		korokke	croquette
gyūdon	a bowl of rice with beef	ebi-furai	fried shrimp
		furaido-chikin	fried chicken
yaki-niku	grilled meat		
yasai-itame	sauteed vegetables	sarada	salad
		sūpu	soup
tsukemono	pickles	supagetii	spaghetti
misoshiru	miso soup	piza	pizza
onigiri	rice ball	hanbāgā	hamburger
		sandoitchi	sandwich
tenpura	fried seafood and vegetables	tōsuto	toast
sushi	vinegared rice with raw fish		
udon	Japanese noodles made from wheat flour		
soba	Japanese noodles made from buckwheat flour		
rāmen	Chinese noodles in soup with meat and vegetables		
		kōhii	coffee
yaki-soba	Chinese stir-fried noodles with pork and vegetables	kōcha	black tea
		kokoa	cocoa
okonomiyaki	a type of pancake grilled with meat, vegetables and egg	jūsu	juice
		kōra	cola

IV. Grammar Explanation

1. Saying numbers

1) *hitotsu, futatsu……tō*
   These words are used to count things up to ten. Eleven and higher are counted by using the numbers themselves.

2) Counter Suffixes
   When counting some sorts of things or expressing the quantity of things, counter suffixes are attached after the numbers.

   - *-nin*   number of people except for one and two

     hitori and *futari* are used for one and two. *4-nin* (four people) is read *yo-nin*.

   - *-dai*   number of machines or vehicles like cars and bicycles
   - *-mai*   number of thin or flat things such as paper, dishes, shirts, CDs, etc.
   - *-kai*   times
   - *-fun*   minutes
   - *-jikan*   hours
   - *-nichi*   days

     The number of days takes the counter suffix *-nichi*. However, from two to ten, the same words as used for dates are used. ("One day" is *1-nichi*, "two days" is *futsuka*, ……, "ten days" is *tōka*.)

   - *-shūkan* weeks
   - *-kagetsu* months
   - *-nen*   years

   Details and other counter suffixes are listed in the appendices.

3) Usage
   Quantifiers (numbers with counter suffixes) are usually put before the verbs they modify. However, this is not always the case with length of time.

   ① Ringo o yottsu kaimashita.   We bought four apples.

   ② Gaikokujin no gakusei ga futari imasu. There are two foreign students.

   ③ Kuni de 2-kagetsu Nihon-go o benkyō-shimashita.
      I studied Japanese for two months in my country.

4) Interrogatives

   (1) *ikutsu* is used to ask how many about things which are counted as *hitotsu, futatsu* …….

   ④ Mikan o ikutsu kaimashita ka.
      …Yattsu kaimashita.
      How many mandarin oranges did you buy?
      …I bought eight.

(2) *nan* is used with a counter suffix to ask how many.

⑤ Kono kaisha ni gaikokujin ga nan-nin imasu ka.
　…5-nin imasu.
　How many foreigners are there in this company?
　…There are five.

⑥ Maiban nan-jikan Nihon-go o benkyō-shimasu ka.
　…2-jikan benkyō-shimasu.
　How many hours do you study Japanese every night?
　…Two hours.

(3) *donokurai* is used to ask the length of time something takes. You can use various units of time in the answer.

⑦ Donokurai Nihon-go o benkyō-shimashita ka.
　…3-nen benkyō-shimashita.
　How long did you study Japanese?
　…I studied it for three years.

⑧ Ōsaka kara Tōkyō made donokurai kakarimasu ka.
　…Shinkansen de 2-jikan han kakarimasu.
　How long does it take from Osaka to Tokyo?
　…It takes two and a half hours by Shinkansen.

5) *gurai*

gurai is added after quantifiers to mean "about."

⑨ Gakkō ni sensei ga 30-nin gurai imasu.
　There are about thirty teachers in our school.

⑩ 15-fun gurai kakarimasu.　　　　　　It takes about fifteen minutes.

2. Quantifier (period) *ni -kai* V

With this expression you can say how often you do something.

⑪ 1-kagetsu ni 2-kai eiga o mimasu.　　I go to see movies twice a month.

3. Quantifier *dake*/N *dake*

dake means "only." It is added after quantifiers or nouns to express that there is no more or nothing (no one) else.

⑫ Pawā-denki ni gaikokujin no shain ga hitori dake imasu.
　There is only one foreign employee in Power Electric.

⑬ Yasumi wa nichi-yōbi dake desu.　　I only have Sundays off.

Lesson 12

I. Vocabulary

kantan[na]	かんたん[な]	easy, simple
chikai	ちかい	near
tōi	とおい	far
hayai	はやい	fast, early
osoi	おそい	slow, late
ōi	おおい	many [people], much
[hito ga ~]	[ひとが~]	
sukunai	すくない	few [people], a little
[hito ga ~]	[ひとが~]	
atatakai	あたたかい	warm
suzushii	すずしい	cool
amai	あまい	sweet
karai	からい	hot (taste), spicy
omoi	おもい	heavy
karui	かるい	light
ii	いい	prefer [coffee]
[kōhii ga ~]	[コーヒーが~]	
kisetsu	きせつ	season
haru	はる	spring
natsu	なつ	summer
aki	あき	autumn, fall
fuyu	ふゆ	winter
tenki	てんき	weather
ame	あめ	rain, rainy
yuki	ゆき	snow, snowy
kumori	くもり	cloudy
hoteru	ホテル	hotel
kūkō	くうこう	airport
umi	うみ	sea, ocean
sekai	せかい	world

pātii	パーティー	party (～o shimasu : give a party)
[o-]matsuri	[お]まつり	festival
shiken	しけん	examination
sukiyaki	すきやき	sukiyaki (beef and vegetable hot pot)
sashimi	さしみ	sashimi (sliced raw fish)
[o-]sushi	[お]すし	sushi (vinegared rice topped with raw fish)
tenpura	てんぷら	tempura (seafood and vegetables deep fried in batter)
ikebana	いけばな	flower arrangement (～o shimasu : practice flower arrangement)
momiji	もみじ	maple, red leaves of autumn
dochira	どちら	which one (between two things)
dochira mo	どちらも	both
zutto	ずっと	by far
hajimete	はじめて	for the first time

◁ Kaiwa ▷

Tadaima.	ただいま。	I'm home.
Okaerinasai.	おかえりなさい。	Welcome home.
Sugoi desu ne.	すごいですね。	That's amazing.
demo	でも	but
Tsukaremashita.	つかれました。	(I'm) tired.

Gion-matsuri	ぎおんまつり	the Gion Festival, the most famous festival in Kyoto
Honkon	ホンコン	Hong Kong
Shingapōru	シンガポール	Singapore
Mainichiya	まいにちや	fictitious supermarket
ABC-sutoa	ABCストア	fictitious supermarket
Japan	ジャパン	fictitious supermarket

II. Translation

Sentence Patterns

1. It was rainy yesterday.
2. It was cold yesterday.
3. Hokkaido is bigger than Kyushu.
4. I like summer best of the year.

Example Sentences

1. Was Kyoto quiet?
   ···No, it wasn't.
2. Was the trip enjoyable?
   ···Yes, it was very enjoyable.
3. Was the weather good?
   ···No, it wasn't so good.
4. How was the party yesterday?
   ···It was very lively. I met various people.
5. Are there more people in Tokyo than in New York?
   ···Yes, a lot more.
6. Which is the faster way to get to the airport, by bus or by train?
   ···The train is faster.
7. Which do you prefer, the sea or the mountains?
   ···I like both.
8. What do you like best of all Japanese dishes?
   ···I like tempura best.

Conversation

How was the Festival?

Miller:	Hello. (I'm home.)
Janitor:	Hello. (Welcome home.)
Miller:	This is a souvenir from Kyoto.
Janitor:	Thank you.
	How was the Gion Festival?
Miller:	It was very interesting.
	There were a lot of foreign visitors.
Janitor:	The Gion Festival is the most famous of all the festivals in Kyoto.
Miller:	Is that so?
Janitor:	Did you take photos?
Miller:	Yes, I took about a hundred photos.
Janitor:	Amazing!
Miller:	Yes. But it made me a bit tired.

III. Reference Words & Information

MATSURI TO MEISHO   FESTIVALS & PLACES OF NOTE

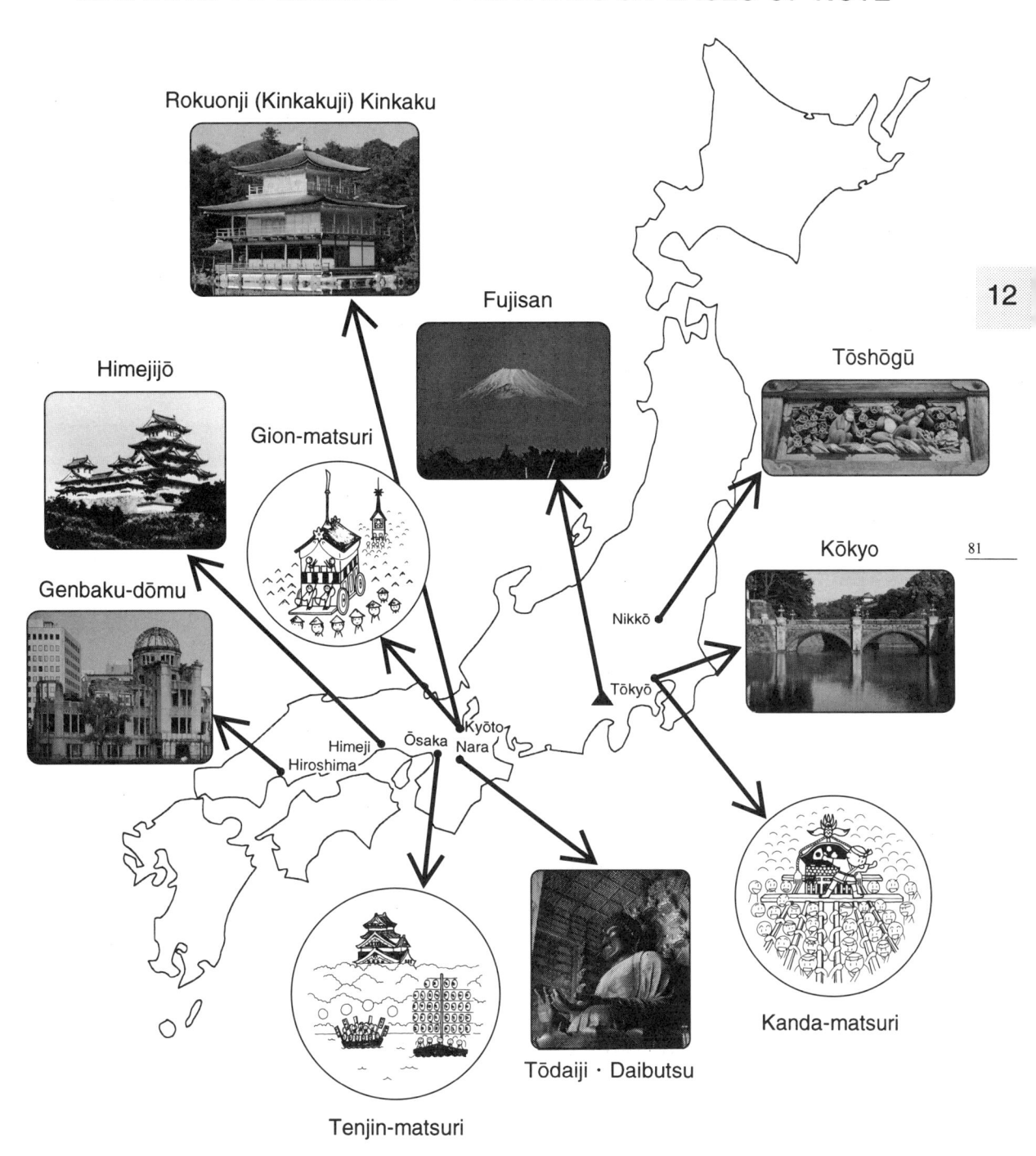

Rokuonji (Kinkakuji) Kinkaku

Himejijō

Gion-matsuri

Fujisan

Tōshōgū

Kōkyo

Genbaku-dōmu

Nikkō

Tōkyō

Himeji
Hiroshima
Ōsaka
Kyōto
Nara

Tenjin-matsuri

Tōdaiji · Daibutsu

Kanda-matsuri

12

81

IV. Grammar Explanation

1. Past tense of noun sentences and *na*-adjective sentences

	non-past (present/future)	past
affirmative	N / *na*-adj : *ame* / *shizuka* } *desu*	N / *na*-adj : *ame* / *shizuka* } *deshita*
negative	N / *na*-adj : *ame* / *shizuka* } *ja arimasen (dewa)*	N / *na*-adj : *ame* / *shizuka* } *ja arimasendeshita (dewa)*

① Kinō wa ame deshita. It was rainy yesterday.

② Kinō no shiken wa kantan ja arimasendeshita.
Yesterday's exam was not easy.

2. Past tense of *i*-adjective sentences

	non-past (present/future)	past
affirmative	*atsui desu*	*atsukatta desu*
negative	*atsukunai desu*	*atsukunakatta desu*

③ Kinō wa atsukatta desu. It was hot yesterday.

④ Kinō no pātii wa amari tanoshikunakatta desu.
I didn't enjoy yesterday's party very much.

3. $\boxed{\text{N}_1 \text{ wa N}_2 \text{ yori adjective } desu}$

This sentence pattern describes the quality and/or state of N₁ in comparison with N₂.

⑤ Kono kuruma wa ano kuruma yori ōkii desu.
This car is bigger than that car.

4. $\boxed{\begin{array}{l}\text{N}_1 \text{ to N}_2 \text{ to dochira ga adjective } desu \text{ ka}\\ \cdots \text{N}_1/\text{N}_2 \text{ no hō ga adjective } desu\end{array}}$

The question asks the listener to choose between two items (N₁ and N₂). The interrogative used is always *dochira* if the comparison is made between two items.

⑥ Sakkā to yakyū to dochira ga omoshiroi desu ka.
···Sakkā no hō ga omoshiroi desu.
Which is more interesting, baseball or football?
···Football is.

⑦ Mirā-san to Santosu-san to dochira ga tenisu ga jōzu desu ka.
   Who is a better tennis player, Mr. Miller or Mr. Santos?

⑧ Hokkaidō to Ōsaka to dochira ga suzushii desu ka.
   Which is cooler, Hokkaido or Osaka?

⑨ Haru to aki to dochira ga suki desu ka.
   Which do you like better, spring or autumn?

5.
>   N₁ [no naka] de { nani / doko / dare / itsu } ga ichiban adjective desu ka
>   ···N₂ ga ichiban adjective desu

This question pattern is used to ask the listener to choose something that is the most "adjective." The choice is made from the group or category denoted by N₁. The interrogative used is decided by the kind of category from which the choice is made.

⑩ Nihon-ryōri [no naka] de nani ga ichiban oishii desu ka.
   ···Tenpura ga ichiban oishii desu.
   Among Japanese dishes, what is the most delicious?
   ···Tempura is.

⑪ Yōroppa de doko ga ichiban yokatta desu ka.
   ···Suisu ga ichiban yokatta desu.
   In Europe, where did you like best?
   ···I liked Switzerland best.

⑫ Kazoku de dare ga ichiban se ga takai desu ka.
   ···Otōto ga ichiban se ga takai desu.
   Who is the tallest of your family?
   ···My younger brother is.

⑬ 1-nen de itsu ga ichiban samui desu ka.
   ···2-gatsu ga ichiban samui desu.
   When is the coldest time of a year?
   ···It's coldest in February.

[Note] When the subject is an interrogative, the particle *ga* is used. (See Lesson 10, *nani ga arimasu ka/dare ga imasu ka*.)

When the subject of an adjective sentence is questioned, *ga* is attached to the interrogative in the same way.

Lesson 13

I. Vocabulary

asobimasu	あそびます	enjoy oneself, play
oyogimasu	およぎます	swim
mukaemasu	むかえます	go to meet, welcome
tsukaremasu	つかれます	get tired
dashimasu	だします	send [a letter]
[tegami o ~]	[てがみを~]	
hairimasu	はいります	enter [a coffee shop]
[kissaten ni ~]	[きっさてんに~]	
demasu	でます	go out [of a coffee shop]
[kissaten o ~]	[きっさてんを~]	
kekkon-shimasu	けっこんします	marry, get married
kaimono-shimasu	かいものします	do shopping
shokuji-shimasu	しょくじします	have a meal, dine
sanpo-shimasu	さんぽします	take a walk [in a park]
[kōen o ~]	[こうえんを~]	
taihen[na]	たいへん[な]	hard, tough, severe, awful
hoshii	ほしい	want (something)
sabishii	さびしい	lonely
hiroi	ひろい	wide, spacious
semai	せまい	narrow, small (room, etc.)
shiyakusho	しやくしょ	municipal office, city hall
pūru	プール	swimming pool
kawa	かわ	river
keizai	けいざい	economy
bijutsu	びじゅつ	fine arts
tsuri	つり	fishing (~o shimasu : fish, angle)
sukii	スキー	skiing (~o shimasu : ski)
kaigi	かいぎ	meeting, conference
		(~o shimasu : hold a conference)
tōroku	とうろく	registration (~o shimasu : register)

shūmatsu	しゅうまつ	weekend
～ goro	～ごろ	about (time)
nanika	なにか	something
dokoka	どこか	somewhere, some place
Onaka ga sukimashita.	おなかが すきました。	(I'm) hungry.
Onaka ga ippai desu.	おなかが いっぱいです。	(I'm) full.
Nodo ga kawakimashita.	のどが かわきました。	(I'm) thirsty.
Sō desu ne.	そうですね。	I agree with you.
Sō shimashō.	そう しましょう。	Let's do that. (used when agreeing with someone's suggestion)

◀ Kaiwa ▶

Go-chūmon wa?	ごちゅうもんは？	May I take your order?
teishoku	ていしょく	set meal
gyūdon	ぎゅうどん	bowl of rice topped with beef
[Shōshō] o-machi kudasai.	[しょうしょう] おまちください。	Please wait [a moment].
betsubetsu ni	べつべつに	separately

Roshia	ロシア	Russia
Tsuruya	つるや	fictitious Japanese restaurant
Ohayō-terebi	おはようテレビ	fictitious TV program

II. Translation

Sentence Patterns
1. I want a personal computer.
2. I want to eat tempura.
3. I will go to France to study cooking.

Example Sentences
1. What do you want most now?
   ···I want a house.
2. Where do you want to go on summer vacation?
   ···I want to go to Okinawa.
3. Because I am tired today, I don't want to do anything.
   ···Me, too. Today's meeting was tough, wasn't it?
4. What will you do this weekend?
   ···I will go to Kobe with my children to see the ships.
5. What did you come to Japan to study?
   ···I came here to study economics.
6. Did you go anywhere on winter vacation?
   ···Yes, I did.
   Where did you go?
   ···I went to Hokkaido to ski.

Conversation
Charge us separately

Yamada:	Why, it's already twelve. Shall we go for lunch?
Miller:	Sure.
Yamada:	Where shall we go?
Miller:	Let me see. Today I want to eat Japanese food.
Yamada:	Then, let's go to "Tsuru-ya."
----------	--
Waiter:	May I take your order?
Miller:	I'll have the tempura set lunch.
Yamada:	I'll have the gyudon.
Waiter:	One tempura set lunch and one gyudon. I'll be right back.
----------	--
Cashier:	1,680 yen altogether, sir.
Miller:	Excuse me. Please charge us separately.
Cashier:	Right. 980 yen for the tempura set lunch, 700 yen for the gyudon.

III. Reference Words & Information

MACHI NO NAKA   TOWN

hakubutsukan	museum	shiyakusho	city hall
bijutsukan	art museum	keisatsusho	police
toshokan	library	kōban	police box
eigakan	movie theater	shōbōsho	fire station
dōbutsuen	zoo	chūshajō	parking lot
shokubutsuen	botanical garden		
yūenchi	amusement park	daigaku	university
		kōkō	senior high school
o-tera	Buddhist temple	chūgakkō	junior high school
jinja	Shinto shrine	shōgakkō	elementary school
kyōkai	Christian church	yōchien	kindergarten
mosuku	Mosque		
		niku-ya	butcher's shop
taiikukan	gymnasium	pan-ya	bakery
pūru	swimming pool	sakana-ya	fishmonger's
kōen	park	sakaya	liquor shop
		yaoya	vegetable shop
taishikan	embassy		
nyūkoku	immigration bureau	kissaten	coffee shop
-kanrikyoku		konbini	convenience store
		sūpā	supermarket
		depāto	department store

IV. Grammar Explanation

1. N *ga hoshii desu*

   This sentence pattern is used to express the speaker's desire to possess or have an object. It can also be used to ask what the listener wants. The object is marked with the particle *ga*. *hosii* is an *i*-adjective.

   ① Watashi wa tomodachi ga hoshii desu.　　I want a friend.
   ② Ima nani ga ichiban hoshii desu ka.　　What do you want most now?
   　　…Kuruma ga hoshii desu.　　…I want a car most.
   ③ Kodomo ga hoshii desu ka.　　Do you want a child?
   　　…Iie, hoshikunai desu.　　…No, I don't.

2. V *masu*-form *tai desu*

   1) Verb *masu*-form

   The form of a verb when it is used with *masu* is called the *masu*-form. In the word *kaimasu*, *kai* is the *masu*-form.

   2) V *masu*-form *tai desu*

   This expresses the speaker's desire to do something. It is also used to ask what the listener wants to do. In this expression, as is seen in ⑤ below, the particle *ga* can replace the particle *o*. The other particles cannot be replaced by *ga*. V *masu*-form *tai* inflects as an *i*-adjective.

   ④ Watashi wa Okinawa e ikitai desu.　　I want to go to Okinawa.
   ⑤ Watashi wa tenpura o tabetai desu.　　I want to eat tempura.
   　　　　　　　　(ga)
   ⑥ Kōbe de nani o kaitai desu ka.　　What do you want to buy in Kobe?
   　　　　　(ga)
   　　…Kutsu o kaitai desu.　　…I want to buy a pair of shoes.
   　　　　　(ga)
   ⑦ Onakaga itai desu kara, nani mo tabetakunai desu.
   　　Because I have a stomachache, I don't want to eat anything.

   [Note 1] *hoshii desu* or ~*tai desu* cannot be used to describe the third person's desire.

   [Note 2] You can neither use *hoshii desu ka* nor V *masu*-form *tai desu ka* when you offer something or invite someone to do something. For example, when you offer a cup of coffee (or invite the listener to have a cup of coffee), you should not say, *kōhii ga hoshii desu ka*, nor should you say *kōhii o nomitai desu ka*. Expressions such as *kōhii wa ikaga desu ka* or *kōhii o nomimasen ka* should be used.

3.

$$\boxed{\text{N(place) } e \begin{Bmatrix} \text{V } \textit{masu}\text{-form} \\ \text{N} \end{Bmatrix} \textit{ni ikimasu/kimasu/kaerimasu}}$$

The purpose for *ikimasu*, *kimasu* or *kaerimasu* is expressed using this pattern. The purpose is marked with the particle *ni*. A noun used before *ni* is of the kind denoting an action.

⑧ Kōbe e Indo-ryōri o tabe ni ikimasu.
  I'm going to Kobe to eat Indian food.

⑨ Kōbe e kaimono ni ikimasu.
  I'm going to Kobe for shopping.

⑩ Nihon e bijutsu no benkyō ni kimashita.
  I came to Japan in order to study art.

[Note] You can also use nouns denoting events such as festivals and concerts before *ni*. In this case, the speaker's purpose is to see or enjoy the event.

⑪ Ashita Kyōto no o-matsuri ni ikimasu.
  I'll go to the festival in Kyoto tomorrow.

4.

$\boxed{\text{N } \textit{ni} \text{ V / N } \textit{o} \text{ V}}$

The particle *ni* marks the goal when used with verbs like *hairimasu*, *norimasu* (get on; see Lesson 16), etc. The particle *o* marks the starting point or place when used with verbs like *demasu*, *orimasu* (get off; see Lesson 16), etc.

⑫ Ano kissaten ni hairimashō.   Let's go in that coffee shop.
⑬ 7-ji ni uchi o demasu.   I leave my house at 7 o'clock.

5. *dokoka/nanika*

dokoka means anywhere or somewhere. *nanika* means anything or something. The particles *e* and *o* can be omitted.

⑭ Fuyu-yasumi wa dokoka [e] ikimashita ka.
  ···Hai, ikimashita.
  Did you go anywhere in the winter vacation?
  ···Yes, I did.

⑮ Nodo ga kawakimashita kara, nanika [o] nomitai desu.
  I'm thirsty. I want to drink something.

6. *go-chūmon*

go is a prefix added to some words to express respect.

⑯ Go-chūmon wa?   May I have your order?

Lesson 14

I. Vocabulary

tsukemasu II	つけます	turn on
keshimasu I	けします	turn off
akemasu II	あけます	open
shimemasu II	しめます	close, shut
isogimasu I	いそぎます	hurry
machimasu I	まちます	wait
tomemasu II	とめます	stop, park
magarimasu I [migi e ~]	まがります [みぎへ ~]	turn [to the right]
mochimasu I	もちます	hold
torimasu I	とります	take, pass
tetsudaimasu I	てつだいます	help (with a task)
yobimasu I	よびます	call
hanashimasu I	はなします	speak, talk
misemasu II	みせます	show
oshiemasu II [jūsho o ~]	おしえます [じゅうしょを ~]	tell [an address]
hajimemasu II	はじめます	start, begin
furimasu I [ame ga ~]	ふります [あめが ~]	rain
kopii-shimasu III	コピーします	copy
eakon	エアコン	air conditioner
pasupōto	パスポート	passport
namae	なまえ	name
jūsho	じゅうしょ	address
chizu	ちず	map
shio	しお	salt
satō	さとう	sugar
yomi-kata	よみかた	how to read, way of reading
~ kata	~かた	how to ~, way of ~ ing

yukkuri	ゆっくり	slowly, leisurely
sugu	すぐ	immediately
mata	また	again
ato de	あとで	later
mō sukoshi	もう すこし	a little more
mō ～	もう ～	～ more, another ～
Ii desu yo.	いいですよ。	Sure./Certainly.
sā	さあ	right (used when encouraging some course of action)
Are?	あれ？	Oh! (in surprise or in wonder)

◁ Kaiwa ▷

Shingō o migi e magatte kudasai.	しんごうを みぎへ まがって ください。	Turn to the right at the signal.
massugu	まっすぐ	straight
Kore de onegai-shimasu.	これで おねがいします。	I'd like to pay with this.
otsuri	おつり	change

~~~~~~~~~~~~~~~~~~~~~~~~~~~~~~

Umeda	うめだ	name of a town in Osaka

II. Translation

Sentence Patterns
1. Wait a moment, please.
2. Mr. Miller is making a telephone call now.

Example Sentences
1. Please write your name and address here.
   ···Yes.

2. Please show me that shirt.
   ···Here you are.
   Do you have one a little bigger?
   ···Yes. How about this shirt?

3. Excuse me. Please tell me how to read this kanji?
   ···It's "kakitome."

4. It's hot, isn't it? Shall I open the window?
   ···Yes, please.

5. Shall I come to the station to pick you up?
   ···No, thank you. I will come by taxi.

6. Where is Ms. Sato?
   ···She is talking with Mr. Matsumoto in the meeting room.
   Then, I will come again later.

Conversation

To Umeda, please

Karina:	To Umeda, please.
Driver:	Yes.

Karina:	Excuse me. Turn to the right at that traffic light.
Driver:	To the right?
Karina:	Yes.

Driver:	Go straight?
Karina:	Yes, go straight.

Karina:	Stop in front of that flower shop.
Driver:	Yes.
	1,800 yen, please.
Karina:	Here you are.
Driver:	That's 3,200 yen change. Thank you.

III. Reference Words & Information

EKI   STATION

kippu-uriba	ticket office, ticket area	tokkyū	super-express train
jidō-kenbaiki	ticket machine	kyūkō	express train
seisanki	fare adjustment machine	kaisoku	rapid service train
kaisatsuguchi	wicket, ticket barrier	junkyū	semi-express train
deguchi	exit	futsū	local train
iriguchi	entrance		
higashi-guchi	east exit	jikokuhyō	timetable
nishi-guchi	west exit	~ hatsu	departing ~
minami-guchi	south exit	~ chaku	arriving at ~
kita-guchi	north exit	[Tōkyō-]iki	for [TOKYO]
chūō-guchi	central exit		
		teikiken	commutation ticket, commuter pass
[puratto]hōmu	platform	kaisūken	coupon ticket
baiten	kiosk	katamichi	one way
koin-rokkā	coin locker	ōfuku	round trip
takushii-noriba	taxi stand		
basu-tāminaru	bus terminal		
basutei	bus stop		

14

93

IV. Grammar Explanation

1. Verb conjugation

    Verbs in Japanese change their forms, i.e., they conjugate, and they are divided into three groups according to the type of conjugation. Depending on the following phrases, you can make sentences with various meanings.

2. Verb groups

    1) Group I verbs

    In the verbs of this group, the last sound of the *masu*-form is that of the *i*-line. (See Main Textbook, p. 2, "Kana to Haku.")

        ka*ki*masu   write   no*mi*masu   drink

    2) Group II verbs

    In most of the verbs of this group, the last sound of the *masu*-form is that of the *e*-line, but in some verbs the last sound of the *masu*-form is that of the *i*-line.

        ta*be*masu   eat   mi*se*masu   show   *mi*masu   see

    3) Group III verbs

    Verbs of this group include *shimasu* and "noun denoting an action + *shimasu*" as well as *kimasu*.

3. Verb *te*-form

    The verb form which ends with *te* or *de* is called the *te*-form. How to make the *te*-form of a verb depends on which group the verb belongs to as explained below. (See Main Textbook, Lesson 14, p. 116, *Renshū* A 1.)

    1) Group I   Depending on the last sound of the *masu*-form, the *te*-form of the verbs of this group is made as shown in the form table. (See Main Textbook, Lesson 14, *Renshū* A 1.) Note that the *te*-form of the verb *ikimasu*, *itte*, is an exception.

    2) Group II   Attach *te* to the *masu*-form.

    3) Group III   Attach *te* to the *masu*-form.

4. ⎡V *te*-form *kudasai*⎦   Please do...

    This sentence pattern is used to ask, instruct or encourage the listener to do something. Naturally, if the listener is one's superior, this expression cannot be used for giving instructions to him/her. The sentences shown below are examples of asking, instructing and encouraging, respectively.

    ① Sumimasen ga, kono kanji no yomi-kata o oshiete kudasai.

       Excuse me, could you tell me how to read this kanji, please?

    ② Koko ni jūsho to namae o kaite kudasai.

       Please write your name and address here.

    ③ Zehi asobi ni kite kudasai.   Please come to my place. (L. 25)

When it is used to ask the listener to do something, *sumimasen ga* is often added before V*te*-form *kudasai* as in ①. This expression is politer than only saying V*te*-form *kudasai*.

5. | V *te*-form *imasu* | be V-ing

   This sentence pattern indicates that a certain action or motion is in progress.

   ④ Mirā-san wa ima denwa o kakete imasu.
      Mr. Miller is making a phone call now.

   ⑤ Ima ame ga futte imasu ka.   Is it raining now?
      ···Hai, futte imasu.   ···Yes, it is.
      ···Iie, futte imasen.   ···No, it is not.

6. | V *masu*-form *mashō ka* | Shall I...?

   This expression is used when the speaker is offering to do something for the listener.

   ⑥ A : Ashita mo kimashō ka.   Shall I come tomorrow, too?
      B : Ē, 10-ji ni kite kudasai.   ···Yes, please come at ten.

   ⑦ A : Kasa o kashimashō ka.   Shall I lend you an umbrella?
      B : Sumimasen. Onegai-shimasu.   ···Yes, please.

   ⑧ A : Nimotsu o mochimashō ka.   Shall I carry your parcel?
      B : Iie, kekkō desu.   ···No, thank you.

   In the above example conversations, B demonstrates how to politely ask or instruct someone to do something (⑥), to accept an offer with gratitude (⑦) and to decline an offer politely (⑧).

7. | S₁ *ga*, S₂ | ..., but...

   ⑨ Shitsurei desu ga, o-namae wa?
      Excuse me, but may I have your name? (L.1)

   ⑩ Sumimasen ga, shio o totte kudasai.   Please pass me the salt.

   You learned the conjunctive particle *ga* in Lesson 8. In expressions such as *shitsurei desu ga* or *sumimasen ga*, which are used as introductory remarks when speaking to someone, *ga*, losing its original meaning, is used to connect two sentences lightly.

8. | N *ga* V |

   When describing a natural phenomenon, the subject is indicated by *ga*.

   ⑪ Ame ga futte imasu.   It is raining.

Lesson 15

I. Vocabulary

tachimasu I	たちます	stand up
suwarimasu I	すわります	sit down
tsukaimasu I	つかいます	use
okimasu I	おきます	put
tsukurimasu I	つくります	make, produce
urimasu I	うります	sell
shirimasu I	しります	get to know
sumimasu I	すみます	be going to live
kenkyū-shimasu III	けんきゅうします	do research
shitte imasu	しって います	know
sunde imasu	すんで います	live [in Osaka]
[Ōsaka ni ~]	[おおさかに ~]	
shiryō	しりょう	materials, data
katarogu	カタログ	catalog
jikokuhyō	じこくひょう	timetable
fuku	ふく	clothes
seihin	せいひん	products
sofuto	ソフト	software
senmon	せんもん	speciality, field of study
haisha	はいしゃ	dentist, dentist's
tokoya	とこや	barber, barber's
pureigaido	プレイガイド	(theater) ticket agency
dokushin	どくしん	single, unmarried

◁ Kaiwa ▷

tokuni	とくに	especially
omoidashimasu I	おもいだします	remember, recollect
go-kazoku	ごかぞく	your family
irasshaimasu I	いらっしゃいます	be (honorific equivalent of *imasu*)
kōkō	こうこう	senior high school

〰〰〰〰〰〰〰〰〰〰〰〰

Nipponbashi	にっぽんばし	name of a shopping district in Osaka

II. Translation

Sentence Patterns
1. You may take photographs.
2. Mr. Santos has a personal computer.

Example Sentences
1. May I keep this catalog?
   ···Sure, please do.
2. May I borrow this dictionary?
   ···I'm sorry, but... I'm using it now.
3. You must not play here.
   ···All right.
4. Do you know the phone number of the City Hall?
   ···No, I don't.
5. Where do you live, Ms. Maria?
   ···I live in Osaka.
6. Is Mr. Wang single?
   ···No, he is married.
7. What is your job?
   ···I am a teacher. I teach at Fuji University.
   Your speciality?
   ···It's Japanese fine art.

Conversation
Tell me about your family

Miller:	Today's movie was good, wasn't it?
Kimura:	Yes, it was. The father was particularly good, wasn't he?
Miller:	Yes. I was reminded of my family.
Kimura:	Were you? Tell me about your family, Mr. Miller.
Miller:	I have my parents and an elder sister.
Kimura:	Where do they live?
Miller:	My parents live near New York City. My sister is in London. How about your family, Ms. Kimura?
Kimura:	There are three of us. My father works for a bank. My mother teaches English at a high school.

III. Reference Words & Information

SHOKUGYŌ   OCCUPATIONS

kaishain company employee	**kōmuin** civil servant	**ekiin** station clerk	**ginkōin** bank clerk	**yūbinkyokuin** postman
ten'in shop clerk	**chōrishi** cook	**riyōshi** barber / **biyōshi** beautician	**kyōshi** teacher	**bengoshi** lawyer
kenkyūsha research worker	**isha/kangofu** doctor/nurse	**untenshu** driver	**keisatsukan** policeman	**gaikōkan** diplomat
seijika politician	**gaka** painter	**sakka** author	**ongakuka** musician	**kenchikuka** architect
enjinia engineer	**dezainā** designer	**jānarisuto** journalist	**kashu/haiyū** singer/actor actress	**supōtsu-senshu** athlete

15

99

IV. Grammar Explanation

1. **V *te*-form *mo ii desu***   You may do...

   This expression is used to grant permission.

   ① Shashin o totte mo ii desu.   You may take pictures.

   To ask for permission, the question form of this sentence is used.

   ② Tabako o sutte mo ii desu ka.   May I smoke?

   How to answer such a question using the same sentence pattern is as follows. Note that an euphemistic answer is given when permission is not granted.

   ③ Kono katarogu o moratte mo ii desu ka.
       ···Ē, ii desu yo. Dōzo.
       ···Sumimasen. Chotto.
     May I have this catalogue?
     ···Yes. Here you are.
     ···Sorry. I'm afraid not.

2. **V *te*-form *wa ikemasen***   You must not do...

   This sentence pattern is used to express prohibition.

   ④ Koko de tabako o sutte wa ikemasen. Kin'en desu kara.
      You must not smoke here. Because this is no-smoking area.

   When you strongly wish to refuse permission to questions using the expression V*te*-form *mo ii desu ka*, you answer *iie, ikemasen*, omitting V*te*-form *wa*. This expression cannot be used by an inferior to a superior.

   ⑤ Sensei, koko de asonde mo ii desu ka.   May we play here, Ma'am?
      ···Iie, ikemasen.   ···No, you must not.

3. **V *te*-form *imasu***

   In addition to the usage of V*te*-form *imasu* you learned in Lesson 14, it is also used in describing a certain continuing state which resulted from a certain action in the past.

   ⑥ Watashi wa kekkon-shite imasu.   I'm married.
   ⑦ Watashi wa Tanaka-san o shitte imasu.   I know Mr. Tanaka.
   ⑧ Watashi wa Ōsaka ni sunde imasu.   I live in Osaka.
   ⑨ Watashi wa kamera o motte imasu.   I have a camera.

   motte imasu means "be holding" and "possess" as well.

4. V te-form *imasu*

V *te*-form *imasu* is also used in describing a habitual action; that is, when the same action is repeatedly performed over a period of time.

Therefore, one's occupation can be expressed by this sentence pattern, like in ⑫ and ⑬. So if the question *o-shigoto wa nan desu ka* is asked, this sentence pattern can be used to answer it.

⑩ IMC wa konpyūtā-sofuto o tsukutte imasu.
   IMC makes computer software.

⑪ Sūpā de firumu o utte imasu.
   Supermarkets sell films.

⑫ Mirā-san wa IMC de hataraite imasu.
   Mr. Miller works for IMC.

⑬ Imōto wa daigaku de benkyō-shite imasu.
   My younger sister is studying at university.

5. *shirimasen*

The negative form of *shitte imasu* is *shirimasen*.

⑭ Shiyakusho no denwa-bangō o shitte imasu ka.
   ···Hai, shitte imasu.
   ···Iie, shirimasen.
   Do you know the telephone number of the city hall?
   ···Yes, I do.
   ···No, I don't.

Lesson 16

I. Vocabulary

norimasu I	のります	ride, get on [a train]
[densha ni 〜]	[でんしゃに 〜]	
orimasu II	おります	get off [a train]
[densha o 〜]	[でんしゃを 〜]	
norikaemasu II	のりかえます	change (trains, etc.)
abimasu II	あびます	take [a shower]
[shawā o 〜]	[シャワーを 〜]	
iremasu II	いれます	put in, insert
dashimasu I	だします	take out, withdraw
hairimasu I	はいります	enter [university]
[daigaku ni 〜]	[だいがくに 〜]	
demasu II	でます	graduate from [university]
[daigaku o 〜]	[だいがくを 〜]	
yamemasu II	やめます	quit or retire from [a company], stop, give up
[kaisha o 〜]	[かいしゃを 〜]	
oshimasu I	おします	push, press
wakai	わかい	young
nagai	ながい	long
mijikai	みじかい	short
akarui	あかるい	bright, light
kurai	くらい	dark
se ga takai	せが たかい	tall (referring to person)
atama ga ii	あたまが いい	clever, smart
karada	からだ	body
atama	あたま	head
kami	かみ	hair
kao	かお	face
me	め	eye
mimi	みみ	ear
kuchi	くち	mouth
ha	は	tooth
onaka	おなか	stomach
ashi	あし	leg, foot

sābisu	サービス	service
jogingu	ジョギング	jogging (～o shimasu : jog)
shawā	シャワー	shower
midori	みどり	green, greenery
[o-]tera	[お]てら	Buddhist temple
jinja	じんじゃ	Shinto shrine
ryūgakusei	りゅうがくせい	foreign student
－ban	－ばん	number －
dōyatte	どうやって	in what way, how
dono ～	どの ～	which ～ (used for three or more)
[Iie,] mada mada desu.	[いいえ、]まだまだです。	[No,] I still have a long way to go.

◀ Kaiwa ▶

O-hikidashi desu ka.	おひきだしですか。	Are you making a withdrawal?
mazu	まず	first of all
kyasshu-kādo	キャッシュカード	cash dispensing card
anshō-bangō	あんしょうばんごう	personal identification number, PIN
tsugi ni	つぎに	next, as a next step
kingaku	きんがく	amount of money
kakunin	かくにん	confirmation (～shimasu : confirm)
botan	ボタン	button

～～～～～～～～～～～～～～～～～～

JR	ＪＲ	Japan Railway
Ajia	アジア	Asia
Bandon	バンドン	Bandung (in Indonesia)
Berakurusu	ベラクルス	Veracruz (in Mexico)
Furanken	フランケン	Franken (in Germany)
Betonamu	ベトナム	Vietnam
Fue	フエ	Hue (in Vietnam)
Daigaku-mae	だいがくまえ	fictitious bus stop

II. Translation

Sentence Patterns
1. In the morning I go jogging, take a shower and go to the office.
2. We dined at a restaurant after the concert was over.
3. The food is delicious in Osaka.
4. This personal computer is light and handy.

Example Sentences
1. What did you do yesterday?
   ···I went to the library and borrowed some books, and then met a friend.
2. How do you go to your university?
   ···I take a No. 16 bus from Kyoto Station and get off at Daigaku-mae.
3. What are you going to do after getting back to your country?
   ···I will work for my father's company.
4. Which person is Mr. Santos?
   ···He is that tall man with dark hair.
5. What kind of city is Nara?
   ···It is a quiet and beautiful city.
6. Who is that person?
   ···That is Ms. Karina. She is Indonesian, and an overseas student at Fuji University.

Conversation
Tell me how to use this machine

Maria:	Excuse me. Could you tell me how to use this machine?
Bank clerk:	You want to make a withdrawal?
Maria:	Yes.
Bank clerk:	Then, please push this button, first.
Maria:	Yes.
Bank clerk:	Do you have a cash card?
Maria:	Yes, here it is.
Bank clerk:	Put it in here, and enter the code number.
Maria:	Yes.
Bank clerk:	Next, enter the sum.
Maria:	Fifty thousand yen. Five...
Bank clerk:	Push this "Man" and "En." And then push this "Kakunin" button.
Maria:	Got it. Thank you very much.

III. Reference Words & Information

ATM NO TSUKAI-KATA   HOW TO WITHDRAW MONEY

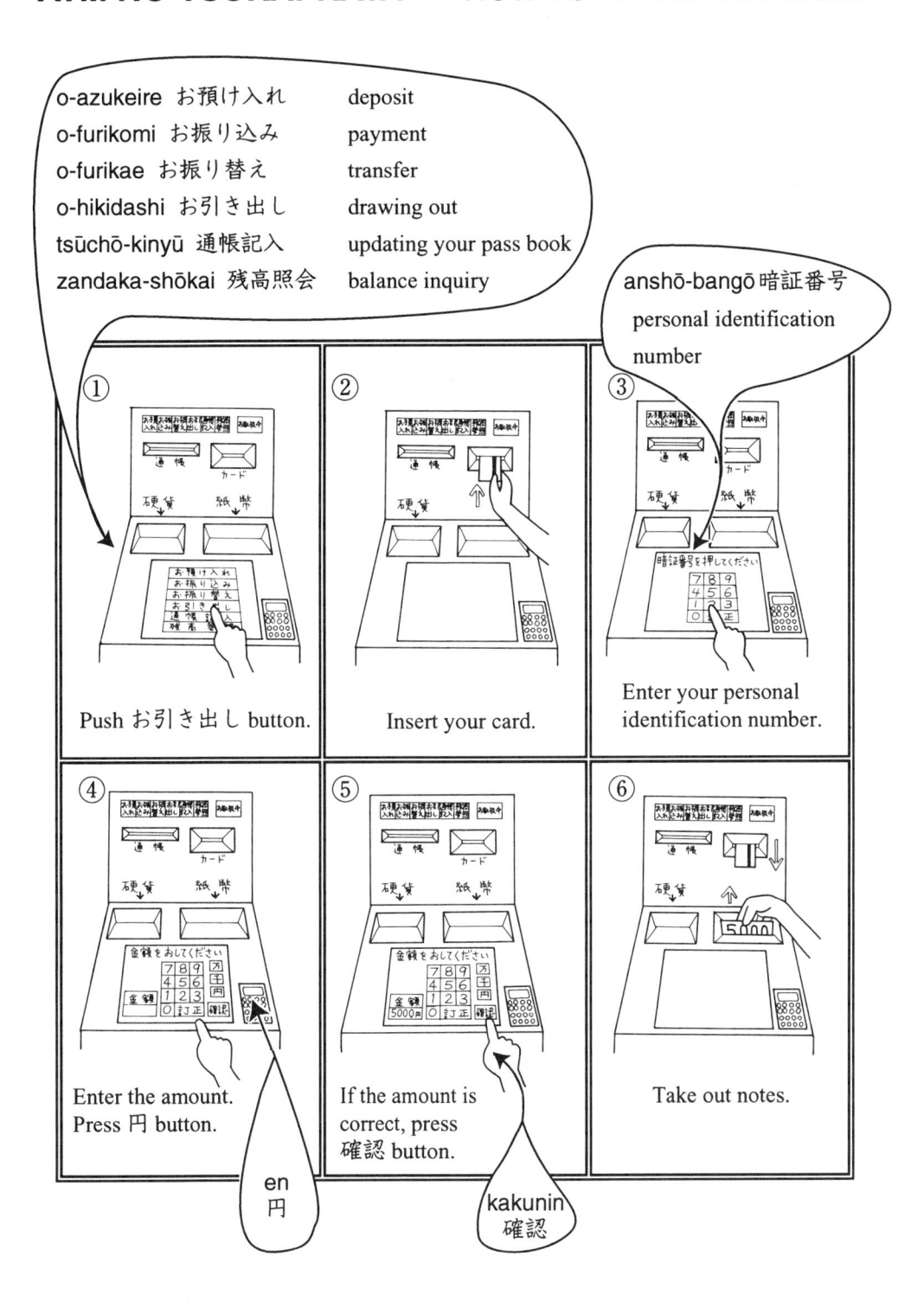

o-azukeire お預け入れ — deposit
o-furikomi お振り込み — payment
o-furikae お振り替え — transfer
o-hikidashi お引き出し — drawing out
tsūchō-kinyū 通帳記入 — updating your pass book
zandaka-shōkai 残高照会 — balance inquiry

anshō-bangō 暗証番号 — personal identification number

① Push お引き出し button.

② Insert your card.

③ Enter your personal identification number.

④ Enter the amount. Press 円 button.

⑤ If the amount is correct, press 確認 button.

⑥ Take out notes.

en 円

kakunin 確認

IV. Grammar Explanation

1. V*te*-form, [V*te*-form], ~

   To connect verb sentences, the *te*-form is used. When two or more actions take place in succession, the actions are mentioned in the order of occurrence by using the *te*-form. The tense of the sentence is determined by the tense form of the last verb in the sentence.

   ① Asa jogingu o shite, shawā o abite, kaisha e ikimasu.
   In the morning, I jog, take a shower and go to the office.

   ② Kōbe e itte, eiga o mite, ocha o nomimashita.
   I went to Kobe, saw a movie and drank tea.

2. *i*-adj (~*i*́) → ~ *kute*,~

   When joining an *i*-adjective sentence to another sentence, take away the *i* from the *i*-adjective and attach *kute*.

ōki - i	→	ōki - kute		big
chiisa - i	→	chiisa - kute		small
i - i	→	*yo - kute	(exception)	good

   ③ Mirā-san wa wakakute, genki desu.
   Mr. Miller is young and lively.

   ④ Kinō wa tenki ga yokute, atsukatta desu.
   Yesterday it was fine and hot.

3. N / *na*-adj [*ná*] } *de*, ~

   When joining noun sentences or *na*-adjective sentences, *desu* is changed to *de*.

   ⑤ Karina-san wa Indoneshia-jin de, Kyōto-daigaku no ryūgakusei desu.
   Ms. Karina is an Indonesian and a student of Kyoto University.

   ⑥ Mirā-san wa hansamu de, shinsetsu desu.
   Mr. Miller is handsome and kind.

   ⑦ Nara wa shizuka de, kireina machi desu.
   Nara is a quiet and beautiful city.

[Note 1] The above structures can be used not only for connecting sentences relating to the same topic but also sentences with different topics.

   ⑧ Karina-san wa gakusei de, Maria-san wa shufu desu.
   Ms. Karina is a student and Maria is a housewife.

[Note 2] This method cannot connect sentences of contradictory notion. In that case, *ga* is used (see Lesson 8, 7).

   × Kono heya wa semakute, kirei desu.
   ○ Kono heya wa semai desu ga, kirei desu. This room is small but clean.

4. V₁ te-form *kara*, V₂

This sentence pattern indicates that upon completion of the action denoted by V₁, the action of V₂ is to be conducted. The tense of the sentence is determined by the tense form of the last verb in the sentence.

⑨ Kuni e kaette kara, chichi no kaisha de hatarakimasu.
   I will work for my father's company after going back to my country.

⑩ Konsāto ga owatte kara, resutoran de shokuji-shimashita.
   We ate at a restaurant after the concert was over.

[Note] The subject of a subordinate clause is indicated by *ga*, as shown in the example sentence ⑩.

5. N₁ *wa* N₂ *ga* adjective

This sentence pattern is used to describe an attribute of a thing or a person. The topic of the sentence is denoted by *wa*. N₁ is the topic of the sentence. N₂ is the subject of the adjective's description.

⑪ Ōsaka wa tabemono ga oishii desu. Food is tasty in Osaka.
⑫ Doitsu no Furanken wa wain ga yūmei desu.
   Franken in Germany produces famous wine.
⑬ Maria-san wa kami ga nagai desu. Maria has long hair.

6. *dōyatte*

dōyatte is used to ask the way or the method of doing something. To answer such a question, the pattern learned in 1. is used.

⑭ Daigaku made dōyatte ikimasu ka.
   ···Kyōto-eki kara 16-ban no basu ni notte, Daigaku-mae de orimasu.
   How do you go to your university?
   ···I take a No.16 bus from Kyoto Station and get off at Daigaku-mae.

7. *dono* N

You learned in Lesson 2 that *kono, sono* and *ano* modify nouns. The interrogative word used in this system is *dono*. *dono* is used to ask the listener to define one among more than two which are concretely presented.

⑮ Santosu-san wa dono hito desu ka.
   ···Ano se ga takakute, kami ga kuroi hito desu.
   Which one is Mr. Santos?
   ···That tall man with black hair is.

Lesson 17

I. Vocabulary

oboemasu II	おぼえます	memorize
wasuremasu II	わすれます	forget
nakushimasu I	なくします	lose
dashimasu I	だします	hand in [a report]
[repōto o ~]	[レポートを ~]	
haraimasu I	はらいます	pay
kaeshimasu I	かえします	give back, return
dekakemasu II	でかけます	go out
nugimasu I	ぬぎます	take off (clothes, shoes, etc.)
motte ikimasu I	もっていきます	take (something)
motte kimasu III	もってきます	bring (something)
shinpai-shimasu III	しんぱいします	worry
zangyō-shimasu III	ざんぎょうします	work overtime
shutchō-shimasu III	しゅっちょうします	go on a business trip
nomimasu I	のみます	take [medicine]
[kusuri o ~]	[くすりを ~]	
hairimasu I	はいります	take [a bath]
[o-furo ni ~]	[おふろに ~]	
taisetsu[na]	たいせつ[な]	important, precious
daijōbu[na]	だいじょうぶ[な]	all right
abunai	あぶない	dangerous
mondai	もんだい	question, problem, trouble
kotae	こたえ	answer
kin'en	きんえん	no smoking
[kenkō-]hokenshō	[けんこう]ほけんしょう	[health] insurance card
kaze	かぜ	cold, flu
netsu	ねつ	fever
byōki	びょうき	illness, disease
kusuri	くすり	medicine

[o-]furo	[お]ふろ	bath
uwagi	うわぎ	jacket, outerwear
shitagi	したぎ	underwear
sensei	せんせい	doctor (used when addressing a medical doctor)
2,3-nichi	2、3にち	a few days
2,3 〜	2、3〜	a few 〜 (〜 is a counter suffix)
〜 made ni	〜までに	before 〜, by 〜 (indicating time limit)
desukara	ですから	therefore, so

◁ Kaiwa ▷

Dō shimashita ka.	どう しましたか。	What's the matter?
[〜 ga] itai desu.	[〜が] いたいです。	(I) have a pain [in my 〜].
nodo	のど	throat
Odaiji ni.	おだいじに。	Take care of yourself. (said to people who are ill)

II. Translation

Sentence Patterns
1. Please don't take photographs here.
2. You must show your passport.
3. You do not have to submit the report.

Example Sentences
1. Do not park your car there, please.
   ···I am sorry.
2. Doctor, may I drink alcohol?
   ···No, refrain from it for two or three days.
   Yes, doctor.
3. Shall we go for a drink tonight?
   ···Sorry. Today I'm going out with my wife.
     So I must go home early.
4. By when do I have to submit the report?
   ···Submit it by Friday, please.
5. Do the children have to pay, too?
   ···No, they don't have to pay.

Conversation
What seems to be the problem?

Doctor:	What seems to be the problem?
Matsumoto:	I have had a sore throat and a slight temperature since yesterday.
Doctor:	Well, please open your mouth.
Doctor:	You have a cold. You need a good rest.
Matsumoto:	Doctor, I have to go to Tokyo on business from tomorrow.
Doctor:	Well then, take this medicine and go to bed early today.
Matsumoto:	Yes, doctor.
Doctor:	And do not take a bath tonight.
Matsumoto:	I see.
Doctor:	Please take care.
Matsumoto:	Thank you very much, doctor.

III. Reference Words & Information

KARADA · BYŌKI   BODY & ILLNESS

Dō shimashita ka.	What seems to be the problem?
atama ga itai	have a headache
onaka ga itai	have a stomachache
ha ga itai	have a toothache
netsu ga aru	have a fever
seki ga deru	have a cough
hanamizu ga deru	have a runny nose
chi ga deru	bleed
hakike ga suru	feel nauseous
samuke ga suru	feel a chill
memai ga suru	feel dizzy
geri o suru	have diarrhea
benpi o suru	be constipated
kega o suru	get injured
yakedo o suru	get burnt
shokuyoku ga nai	have no appetite
kata ga koru	feel stiff in one's shoulders
karada ga darui	feel weary
kayui	itchy

Body labels: kao, atama, me, kami, hana, mimi, kuchi, nodo, kubi, ago, kata, mune, senaka, ude, yubi, te, hiji, tsume, hiza, onaka, koshi, hone, ashi, shiri

		gikkurigoshi	slipped disc
kaze	cold	nenza	sprain
infuruenza	influenza	kossetsu	bone fracture
mōchō	appendicitis	futsukayoi	hangover

IV. Grammar Explanation

1. Verb *nai*-form

   The verb form used with *nai* is called the *nai*-form; that is to say, *kaka* of *kakanai* is the *nai*-form of *kakimasu* (write). How to make the *nai*-form is given below (see Main Textbook, Lesson 17, p. 140, *Renshū* A 1).

   1) Group I
   In the verbs of this group the last sound of the *masu*-form is always the sound in the *i*-line. So, replace it with the sound of the *a*-line to make a *nai*-form. The exceptions to this rule are such verbs as *kaimasu*, *aimasu*, etc. (*wa* is the last sound of the *nai*-form in these verbs instead of *a*.) (See Main Textbook, p. 2, "*Kana to Haku*.")

kaki-masu → kaka-nai	isogi-masu → isoga-nai
yomi-masu → yoma-nai	asobi-masu → asoba-nai
tori-masu → tora-nai	machi-masu → mata-nai
sui-masu → suwa-nai	hanashi-masu → hanasa-nai

   2) Group II
   The *nai*-form of verbs of this group is just the same as the *masu*-form.

   tabe-masu → tabe-nai
   mi-masu → mi-nai

   3) Group III
   The *nai*-form of *shimasu* is the same as the *masu*-form. *kimasu* becomes *ko (nai)*.

   benkyō-shi-masu → benkyō-shi-nai
   shi-masu → shi-nai
   ki-masu → ko-nai

2. V *nai*-form *nai de kudasai*   Please don't...

   This expression is used to ask or instruct someone not to do something.

   ① Watashi wa genki desu kara, shinpai-shinai de kudasai.
      I am fine, so please don't worry about me.
   ② Koko de shashin o toranai de kudasai.
      Please don't take pictures here.

3. V *nai*-form *nakereba narimasen*   must...

   This expression means something has to be done regardless of the will of the actor. Note that this doesn't have a negative meaning.

   ③ Kusuri o nomanakereba narimasen.   I must take medicine.

4. V *nai*-form *nakute mo ii desu*   need not ...

This sentence pattern indicates that the action described by the verb does not have to be done.

④ **Ashita konakute mo ii desu.**   You don't have to come tomorrow.

5. N (object) *wa*

You learned in Lesson 6 that the particle *o* is attached to the direct object of verbs. Here you learn that the object is made a topic by replacing *o* with *wa*.

Koko ni nimotsu o okanai de kudasai.

Please don't put parcels here.

⑤ **Nimotsu wa koko ni okanai de kudasai.**

As for parcels, don't put them here.

Kaisha no shokudō de hirugohan o tabemasu.

I have lunch in the company cafeteria.

⑥ **Hirugohan wa kaisha no shokudō de tabemasu.**

As for lunch, I have it in the company cafeteria.

6. N (time) *made ni* V

The point in time indicated by *made ni* is the time limit by which an action is to be done.

⑦ **Kaigi wa 5-ji made ni owarimasu.**

The meeting will be over by five.

⑧ **Do-yōbi made ni hon o kaesanakereba narimasen.**

I must return the book by Saturday.

[Note] Make sure you do not confuse *made ni* with the particle *made*.

5-ji made hatarakimasu.   I work until five. (L. 4)

Lesson 18

I. Vocabulary

dekimasu II	できます	be able to, can
araimasu I	あらいます	wash
hikimasu I	ひきます	play (stringed instrument or piano, etc.)
utaimasu I	うたいます	sing
atsumemasu II	あつめます	collect, gather
sutemasu II	すてます	throw away
kaemasu II	かえます	exchange, change
unten-shimasu III	うんてんします	drive
yoyaku-shimasu III	よやくします	reserve, book
kengaku-shimasu III	けんがくします	visit some place for study
piano	ピアノ	piano
－mētoru	－メートル	－ meter
kokusai～	こくさい～	international ～
genkin	げんきん	cash
shumi	しゅみ	hobby
nikki	にっき	diary
[o-]inori	[お]いのり	prayer (～o shimasu : pray)
kachō	かちょう	section chief
buchō	ぶちょう	department chief
shachō	しゃちょう	president of a company

◁ Kaiwa ▷

dōbutsu	どうぶつ	animal
uma	うま	horse
hē	へえ	Really! (used when expressing surprise)
Sore wa omoshiroi desu ne.	それは おもしろいですね。	That must be interesting.
nakanaka	なかなか	not easily (used with negatives)
bokujō	ぼくじょう	ranch, stock farm
Hontō desu ka.	ほんとうですか。	Really?
zehi	ぜひ	by all means

~~~~~~~~~~~~~~~~~~~~~~~~~~~~

Biitoruzu	ビートルズ	the Beatles, famous British music group

II. Translation

Sentence Patterns
1. Mr. Miller can read Kanji.
2. My hobby is watching films.
3. I write in my diary before I go to bed.

Example Sentences
1. Can you ski?
   ⋯Yes, I can. But I am not very good at it.
2. Can you use a personal computer, Ms. Maria?
   ⋯No, I can't.
3. Until what time can we visit Osaka Castle?
   ⋯It is open until five o'clock.
4. Can I pay by credit card?
   ⋯I am sorry, but please pay in cash.
5. What is your hobby?
   ⋯Collecting old clocks and watches.
6. Must Japanese children learn Hiragana before they enter school?
   ⋯No, they need not.
7. Please take this medicine before meals.
   ⋯Yes, I will.
8. When did you get married?
   ⋯We got married three years ago.

Conversation
What is your hobby?

Yamada: What is your hobby, Mr. Santos?
Santos: Photography.
Yamada: What kind of photos do you take?
Santos: Photos of animals. I like those of horses, especially.
Yamada: Oh, that's interesting.
Have you taken photos of horses since you came to Japan?
Santos: No.
You can hardly ever see horses in Japan.
Yamada: There is a lot of pastureland for horses in Hokkaido.
Santos: Really?
Then I would really like to go there on summer vacation.

III. Reference Words & Information

UGOKI   ACTIONS

tobu fly	tobu jump	noboru climb	hashiru run
oyogu swim	moguru dive	tobikomu dive into	sakadachi-suru stand upside down
hau crawl	keru kick	furu wave	mochiageru lift
nageru throw	tataku pat	hiku pull	osu push
mageru bend	nobasu extend	korobu fall down	furimuku look back

18

117

IV. Grammar Explanation

1. Verb dictionary form

    This form is the basic form of a verb. Verbs are given in this form in the dictionary, hence the name. How to make the dictionary form is given below. (See Main Textbook, Lesson 18, p. 148, *Renshū* A 1.)

    1) Group I   In the verbs of this group the last sound of the *masu*-form is always in the *i*-line. Replace it with the sound in the *u*-line to make the dictionary form. (See Main Textbook, p. 2, "*Kana to Haku*.")
    2) Group II Attach *ru* to the *masu*-form.
    3) Group III *shimasu* becomes *suru* and *kimasu* becomes *kuru*.

2. | N | | |
   | V dictionary form *koto* | *ga dekimasu* | can... |

    dekimasu is the verb which expresses ability or possibility. A noun and V dictionary form *koto* before *ga* indicates the content of ability or possibility.

    1) Noun

    Nouns placed before *ga* are mostly nouns which express actions such as driving a car, shopping, skiing, dancing, etc. Nouns such as *Nihon-go*, which is associated with the action *hanasu*, or *piano*, which is associated with the action *hiku*, can also be used here.

    ① Mirā-san wa Nihon-go ga dekimasu.
       Mr. Miller can speak Japanese.

    ② Yuki ga takusan furimashita kara, kotoshi wa sukii ga dekimasu.
       It's snowed a lot, so we can ski this year.

    2) Verb

    When a verb is used to describe ability or possibility, *koto* should be attached to the dictionary form of the verb to make it a nominalized phrase and then *ga dekimasu* is put after that.

    ③ Mirā-san wa <u>kanji o yomu koto</u> ga dekimasu.
                   nominalized phrase   Mr. Miller can read Kanji.

    ④ <u>Kādo de harau koto</u> ga dekimasu.   You can pay by credit card.
       nominalized phrase

3. | *Watashi no shumi wa* { N / V dictionary form *koto* } *desu* | My hobby is... |

    As shown in ⑤ and ⑥ below, V dictionary form *koto* can express the content of hobbies more concretely than the noun alone can do.

    ⑤ Watashi no shumi wa <u>ongaku</u> desu.   My hobby is music.

    ⑥ Watashi no shumi wa <u>ongaku o kiku koto</u> desu.
       My hobby is listening to the music.

4.
| V₁ dictionary form |
| N *no* | *mae ni*, V₂ | ..., before...
| Quantifier (period) |

1) Verb

This sentence pattern indicates that the action of V₂ occurs before the action of V₁ takes place. Even when the tense of V₂ is in the past tense or the future tense, V₁ is always in the dictionary form.

⑦ Nihon e kuru mae ni, Nihon-go o benkyō-shimashita.
   I studied Japanese before I came to Japan.

⑧ Neru mae ni, hon o yomimasu.   I read a book before I go to bed.

2) Noun

When *mae ni* comes after a noun, the particle *no* is put between the noun and *mae ni*. Nouns before *mae ni* are nouns which express actions or nouns which imply actions.

⑨ Shokuji no mae ni, te o araimasu.   I wash my hands before eating.

3) Quantifier (period)

When *mae ni* comes after a quantifier (period), the particle *no* is not necessary.

⑩ Tanaka-san wa 1-jikan mae ni, dekakemashita.
   Mr. Tanaka left an hour ago.

5. *nakanaka*

When *nakanaka* is accompanied by a negative expression, it means "not easily" or "not as expected."

⑪ Nihon de wa nakanaka uma o miru koto ga dekimasen.
   In Japan we can rarely see horses.

[Note] *wa* of *Nihon de wa* in ⑪ is attached to *de* to emphasize the location or area under discussion.

6. *zehi*

zehi is used with expressions of hope and request such as *hoshii desu*, V*masu*-form *tai desu* and V *te*-form *kudasai* and emphasizes the meaning of the expressions.

⑫ Zehi Hokkaidō e ikitai desu.
   I want to go to Hokkaido very much.

⑬ Zehi asobi ni kite kudasai.   Please come to my place. (L. 25)

Lesson 19

I. Vocabulary

noborimasu I [yama ni ~]	のぼります [やまに～]	climb [a mountain]
tomarimasu I [hoteru ni ~]	とまります [ホテルに～]	stay [at a hotel]
sōji-shimasu III	そうじします	clean (a room)
sentaku-shimasu III	せんたくします	wash (clothes)
renshū-shimasu III	れんしゅうします	practice
narimasu I	なります	become
nemui	ねむい	sleepy
tsuyoi	つよい	strong
yowai	よわい	weak
chōshi ga ii	ちょうしが いい	be in good condition
chōshi ga warui	ちょうしが わるい	be in bad condition
chōshi	ちょうし	condition
gorufu	ゴルフ	golf (~o shimasu : play golf)
sumō	すもう	sumo wrestling
pachinko	パチンコ	pinball game (~o shimasu : play pachinko)
ocha	おちゃ	tea ceremony
hi	ひ	day, date
ichido	いちど	once
ichido mo	いちども	not once, never (used with negatives)
dandan	だんだん	gradually
mōsugu	もうすぐ	soon
okagesama de	おかげさまで	Thank you. (used when expressing gratitude for help received)

◁ Kaiwa ▷

kanpai	かんぱい	Bottoms up./Cheers!
jitsuwa	じつは	actually, to tell the truth
daietto	ダイエット	diet (~*o shimasu* : go on a diet)
nankai mo	なんかいも	many times
shikashi	しかし	but, however
muri[na]	むり[な]	excessive, impossible
karada ni ii	からだに いい	good for one's health
kēki	ケーキ	cake

~~~~~~~~~~~~~~~~~~~~~~~~~~~~

Katsushika Hokusai	かつしか ほくさい	famous Edo period wood block artist and painter (1760-1849)

19

II. Translation

Sentence Patterns
1. I have been to see sumo.
2. On holidays I play tennis, take walks and so on.
3. It's going to get hotter and hotter from now on.

Example Sentences
1. Have you been to Hokkaido?
   ···Yes, I once have. I went there two years ago with my friends.
2. Have you ever ridden a horse?
   ···No, I never have. I am eager to try it.
3. What did you do on your winter vacation?
   ···I visited temples and shrines in Kyoto, held a party with friends, and so on.
4. What would you like to do in Japan?
   ···I would like to go on a trip, learn the tea ceremony and so on.
5. How are you feeling?
   ···I've got better, thank you.
6. You have become good at Japanese.
   ···Thank you, but I still have a long way to go.
7. Teresa, what would you like to be?
   ···I would like to be a doctor.

Conversation
As for my diet, I'll start it tomorrow

All:	Cheers!
	--
Ms. Matsumoto:	Why, Ms. Maria, you're not eating much.
Maria:	No. To tell the truth, I have been on a diet since yesterday.
Ms. Matsumoto:	Have you? I have tried being on a diet many times, too.
Maria:	What kind of diets have you tried?
Ms. Matsumoto:	I tried eating only apples, and drinking a lot of water, and so on.
Mr. Matsumoto:	I'm afraid strict diets are not good for your health.
Maria:	You are right.
Ms. Matsumoto:	Ms. Maria, this cake is delicious.
Maria:	Is it?
	.... I'll start dieting again tomorrow.

III. Reference Words & Information

DENTŌ-BUNKA · GORAKU   TRADITIONAL CULTURE & ENTERTAINMENT

sadō (ocha) — tea ceremony	kadō (ikebana) — flower arrangement	shodō — calligraphy
kabuki — Kabuki	nō — Noh	bunraku — Bunraku
sumō — sumo	jūdō — judo	kendō — kendo
karate — karate	manzai, rakugo — manzai, rakugo	igo, shōgi — go, shogi
pachinko — pachinko	karaoke — karaoke	bon-odori — Bon dance

IV. Grammar Explanation

1. Verb *ta*-form

In this lesson you learn the *ta*-form. How to make the *ta*-form is shown below. (See Main Textbook, Lesson 19, p. 156, *Renshū* A 1.)

The *ta*-form is made by changing *te* and *de* of the *te*-form into *ta* and *da* respectively.

	te-form	→	*ta*-form
Group I	kai*te*	→	kai*ta*
	non*de*	→	non*da*
Group II	tabe*te*	→	tabe*ta*
Group III	ki*te*	→	ki*ta*
	shi*te*	→	shi*ta*

2. ⎡V *ta*-form *koto ga arimasu*⎤ have the experience of V-ing

This sentence pattern is used to describe what one has experienced in the past. This is basically the same sentence as *watashi wa* N *ga arimasu* which you learned in Lesson 9. The content of one's experience is expressed by the nominalized phrase V *ta*-form *koto*.

① Uma ni notta koto ga arimasu.   I have ridden a horse.

Note that it is, therefore, different from a sentence which merely states the fact that one did something at a certain time in the past.

② Kyonen Hokkaidō de uma ni norimashita.
   I rode a horse in Hokkaido last year.

3. ⎡V *ta*-form *ri*, V *ta*-form *ri shimasu*⎤ V ...and V ..., and so on

You learned an expression for referring to a few things and persons among many (~*ya* ~*[nado]*) in Lesson 10. The sentences learned here are used in referring to some actions among many other actions. The tense of this sentence pattern is shown at the end of the sentence.

③ Nichi-yōbi wa tenisu o shitari, eiga o mitari shimasu.
   On Sundays I play tennis, see a movie and so on.

④ Nichi-yōbi wa tenisu o shitari, eiga o mitari shimashita.
   Last Sunday I played tennis, saw a movie and so on.

[Note] Make sure that you don't confuse the meaning of this sentence pattern with that of the *te*-form sentence (⑤) which you learned in Lesson 16.

⑤ Nichi-yōbi wa tenisu o shite, eiga o mimashita.
   Last Sunday I played tennis and then saw a movie.

In ⑤ it is clear that seeing a movie took place after playing tennis. In ④ there is no time relation between the two activities. These activities are mentioned as example activities among the activities done on Sunday to imply that one did other activities besides them. And it is not natural that actions usually done by everybody every day such as getting up in the morning, taking meals, going to bed at night, etc., are mentioned.

4.
```
i-adj (~i̸) → ~ku
na-adj [n̸a] → ni    } narimasu    become...
N ni
```

narimasu means "become" and indicates changes in a state or condition.

⑥ samui	→	samuku narimasu	get cold
⑦ genki[na]	→	genki ni narimasu	get well
⑧ 25-sai	→	25-sai ni narimasu	become 25 years old

5. *Sō desu ne*

sō desu ne is used when you agree or sympathize with what your partner in conversation said. *sō desu ka* with a falling intonation is a similar expression to this (see Lesson 2, 6). *sō desu ka*(↘) is, however, an expression of your conviction or exclamation after getting information which was unknown to you, while *sō desu ne* is used to express your agreement or sympathy with your partner in conversation when he/she refers to something you agree with or already know.

⑨ Samuku narimashita ne.   It's got cold, hasn't it?
　　⋯Sō desu ne.   ⋯Yes, it has.

Lesson 20

I. Vocabulary

irimasu I [biza ga ~]	いります ［ビザが～］	need, require [a visa]
shirabemasu II	しらべます	check, investigate
naoshimasu I	なおします	repair, correct
shūri-shimasu III	しゅうりします	repair
denwa-shimasu III	でんわします	phone
boku	ぼく	I (an informal equivalent of *watashi* used by men)
kimi	きみ	you (an informal equivalent of *anata* used by men)
~ kun	～くん	Mr. (an informal equivalent of ~*san* used by men)
un	うん	yes (an informal equivalent of *hai*)
uun	ううん	no (an informal equivalent of *iie*)
sarariiman	サラリーマン	salaried worker, office worker
kotoba	ことば	word, language
bukka	ぶっか	commodity prices
kimono	きもの	kimono (traditional Japanese attire)
biza	ビザ	visa
hajime	はじめ	the beginning
owari	おわり	the end
kotchi	こっち	this way, this place (an informal equivalent of *kochira*)
sotchi	そっち	this way, that place (an informal equivalent of *sochira*)
atchi	あっち	this way, that place over there (an informal equivalent of *achira*)
dotchi	どっち	which one (between two things), which way, where (an informal equivalent of *dochira*)

konoaida	このあいだ	the other day
minna de	みんなで	all together
～ kedo	～けど	～, but (an informal equivalent of *ga*)

◀ Kaiwa ▶

Kuni e kaeru no?	くにへ かえるの？	Are you going back to your country?
Dō suru no?	どう するの？	What will you do?
Dō shiyō ka na.	どう しようかな。	What shall I do?
yokattara	よかったら	if you like
iroiro	いろいろ	various

II. Translation

Sentence Patterns
1. Mr. Santos did not come to the party.
2. Things are expensive in Japan.
3. The sea around Okinawa was beautiful.
4. Today is my birthday.

Example Sentences
1. Will you have some ice cream?
   ···Yes, I will.
2. Do you have any scissors?
   ···No, I don't.
3. Did you see Ms. Kimura yesterday?
   ···No, I didn't.
4. Shall we go to Kyoto all together tomorrow?
   ···Yes. That sounds nice.
5. Is the curry delicious?
   ···Yes, it is hot, but delicious.
6. Are you free now?
   ···Yes, I am. Why?
   Give me a hand, please.
7. Do you have a dictionary?
   ···No, I don't.

Conversation
What will you do for the summer vacation?

Kobayashi:	Are you going home for the summer vacation?
Thawaphon:	No, I won't. Though I want to.... What about you, Mr. Kobayashi?
Kobayashi:	Well, what shall I do? Have you climbed Mt. Fuji, Mr. Thawaphon?
Thawaphon:	No, I haven't.
Kobayashi:	Then, if you'd like, shall we go together?
Thawaphon:	Yes, okay. When?
Kobayashi:	How about the beginning of August?
Thawaphon:	Sounds good.
Kobayashi:	Then, I will check up on various things and call you later.
Thawaphon:	Thanks. I'll be waiting.

III. Reference Words & Information

HITO NO YOBI-KATA   HOW TO ADDRESS PEOPLE

Oniichan Onēchan! / hāi / "Taro, Hanako!!"	12-sai / Ā! Sō ka. / Papa, kyō wa Tarō no tanjōbi yo. / "Dear, do you know today is Taro's birthday?"

In families, people call each other from the viewpoint of the youngest of the family. A parent calls his/her eldest son or daughter "oniichan" (elder brother) or "onēchan" (elder sister) respectively, standing in the position of his/her younger sister or brother.

When parents talk in the presence of their children, the husband calls his wife "okāsan" or "mama" (mother), and the wife, her husband "otōsan" or "papa" (father). This practice, however, has been changing recently, and the number of couples who call each other by their names is increasing.

Buchō, sain onegai-shimasu. / "Mr. Matsumoto, may I have your signature?"	O-kyaku-sama, yoku o-niai desu yo. / "The necktie suits you very much, sir (ma'am)"	Sensei, onaka ga itai'n desu. / "Doctor, I have a stomachache."

In society, people call each other by the names of their role in the group to which they belong. At work, a subordinate calls his boss by his job title. At shops a shop assistant calls his/her customer "o-kyaku-sama" (Mr./Ms. customer). Doctors are called "sensei" (teacher) by their patients.

IV. Grammar Explanation

1. Polite style and plain style

Japanese language has two styles of speech: polite style and plain style.

polite style	plain style
Ashita Tōkyō e ikimasu. I will go to Tokyo tomorrow.	*Ashita Tōkyō e iku.* I will go to Tokyo tomorrow.
Mainichi isogashii desu. I am busy every day.	*Mainichi isogashii.* I am busy every day.
Sumō ga suki desu. I like sumo.	*Sumō ga suki da.* I like sumo.
Fujisan ni noboritai desu. I want to climb Mt. Fuji.	*Fujisan ni noboritai.* I want to climb Mt. Fuji.
Doitsu e itta koto ga arimasen. I have never been to Germany.	*Doitsu e itta koto ga nai.* I have never been to Germany.

The predicates which are used in polite style sentences and accompanied by either **desu** or **masu** are called the polite form, while the predicates used in plain style sentences are called the plain form. (See Main Textbook, Lesson 20, p. 166, *Renshū* A 1)

2. Proper use of the polite style or the plain style

1) The polite style can be used at anytime in any place and to anybody. Therefore, the polite style is used most commonly in daily conversation between adults who are not close friends. It is used when talking to a person one has met for the first time, to one's superiors, or even to persons in a similar age group to whom one is not very close. The polite style may be chosen when one talks to a person who is younger or lower in rank yet not so close. The plain style is used when talking to one's close friends, colleagues and family members.
Note that you need to be careful about how much politeness is needed, basing this on the age of your conversation partner and your type of relationship. If the plain style is used inappropriately, you could sound rough and impolite, so when you cannot tell the situation it is safer to use the polite style.

2) The plain style is commonly used in written work. Newspapers, books, theses and diaries are all written in the plain style. Most letters are written in the polite style.

3. Conversation in the plain style

1) Questions in the plain style generally omit the particle *ka*, which denotes a question, and end with a rising intonation, such as *nomu*(↗).

① Kōhii o nomu? (↗)   Do you want a coffee?
   ⋯Un, nomu. (↘)   ⋯Yes, I do.

2) In noun and *na*-adjective questions, *da*, which is the plain form of *desu*, is omitted. In an answer in the affirmative, ending the sentence with *da* could sound too rough. You can either omit *da* or add some sentence final particle to soften the tone of the sentence. Women seldom use *da*.

② Konban hima?   Are you free tonight?
                               (used by both men and women)
   ⋯Un, hima/hima da/hima da yo.   ⋯Yes, I am. (used by men)
   ⋯Un, hima/hima yo.   ⋯Yes, I am. (used by women)
   ⋯Uun, hima ja nai.   ⋯No, I am not.
                               (used by both men and women)

3) In the plain style, certain particles are often omitted if the meaning of the sentence is evident from the context.

③ Gohan [o] taberu?   Will you take a meal?
④ Ashita Kyōto [e] ikanai?
   Won't you come to Kyoto tomorrow with me?
⑤ Kono ringo [wa] oishii ne. This apple is tasty, isn't it?
⑥ Soko ni hasami [ga] aru?   Is there a pair of scissors there?

de, ni, kara, made, to, etc., however, are not omitted because the meaning of the sentence may not be clear without them.

4) In the plain style, *i* of V *te*-form *iru* is also often dropped.

⑦ Jisho, motte [i]ru?   Do you have a dictionary?
   ⋯Un, motte [i]ru.   ⋯ Yes, I do.
   ⋯Uun, motte [i]nai.   ⋯ No, I don't.

5) *kedo*

kedo has the same function as *ga*, which is used to connect two sentences (see Lesson 8, 7 and Lesson 14, 7). It is often used in conversations.

⑧ Sono karē-raisu [wa] oishii?
   ⋯Un, karai kedo, oishii.
   Is that curry and rice tasty?
   ⋯Yes, it's hot but tasty.
⑨ Sumō no chiketto [ga] aru kedo, issho ni ikanai?
   ⋯Ii ne.
   I have tickets for sumo. Won't you come with me.
   ⋯Sure.

Lesson 21

I. Vocabulary

omoimasu I	おもいます	think
iimasu I	いいます	say
tarimasu II	たります	be enough, be sufficient
kachimasu I	かちます	win
makemasu II	まけます	lose, be beaten
arimasu I 　[o-matsuri ga ～]	あります 　[おまつりが～]	[a festival] be held, take place
yaku ni tachimasu I	やくに たちます	be useful
muda[na]	むだ[な]	wasteful
fuben[na]	ふべん[な]	inconvenient
onaji	おなじ	the same
sugoi	すごい	awful, great (expresses astonishment or admiration)
shushō	しゅしょう	prime minister
daitōryō	だいとうりょう	president
seiji	せいじ	politics
nyūsu	ニュース	news
supiichi	スピーチ	speech (～o shimasu: make a speech)
shiai	しあい	game, match
arubaito	アルバイト	side job (～o shimasu: work part time)
iken	いけん	opinion
[o-]hanashi	[お]はなし	talk, speech, what one says, story (～o shimasu: talk, tell a story)
yūmoa	ユーモア	humor
muda	むだ	waste
dezain	デザイン	design
kōtsū	こうつう	transportation, traffic
rasshu	ラッシュ	rush hour

saikin	さいきん	recently, these days
tabun	たぶん	probably, perhaps, maybe
kitto	きっと	surely
hontō ni	ほんとうに	really
sonnani	そんなに	not so much (used with negatives)
〜 ni tsuite	〜に ついて	about 〜, concerning 〜
Shikata ga arimasen.	しかたが ありません。	There is no other choice./It can't be helped.

◁ Kaiwa ▷

Shibaraku desu ne.	しばらくですね。	It's been a long time (since I last saw you)./Long time no see.
〜 demo nomimasen ka.	〜でも のみませんか。	How about drinking 〜 or something?
Minai to …….	みないと……。	I've got to watch it.
mochiron	もちろん	of course

kangarū	カンガルー	kangaroo
Kyaputen Kukku	キャプテン・クック	Captain James Cook (1728 – 79)

II. Translation

Sentence Patterns

1. I think it will rain tomorrow.
2. The prime minister said that he would go to the U.S.A. next month.

Example Sentences

1. Which is more important, work or family?
   ···I think both are important.
2. What do you think of Japan?
   ···I think things are expensive in Japan.
3. Where is Mr. Miller?
   ···I think he is in the meeting room.
4. Does Mr. Miller know this news?
   ···No, I don't think he does.
     He was on a business trip.
5. Has little Teresa fallen asleep yet?
   ···Yes, I think she has.
6. Do you pray before meals?
   ···No, we don't, but we say "Itadakimasu."
7. Did you say something in the meeting?
   ···Yes. I said that a lot of photocopying had been wastefully done.
8. In July there will be a festival in Kyoto, won't there?
   ···Yes, there will be.

Conversation

I think so, too

Matsumoto:	Mr. Santos, it's been a long time.
Santos:	Mr. Matsumoto, how are you?
Matsumoto:	I'm fine. How about going for a beer or something?
Santos:	That sounds good.
-----------	-----------------------------------
Santos:	There will be a soccer game between Japan and Brazil from ten tonight.
Matsumoto:	Yes, there will. I must be sure to watch it. Which team do you think will win?
Santos:	Of course, Brazil.
Matsumoto:	But I tell you recently Japan have got a lot better.
Santos:	I think so, too.... Oh, it's time that we went home.
Matsumoto:	Yes, it is. Let's go home.

III. Reference Words & Information

YAKUSHOKU-MEI   POSITIONS IN SOCIETY

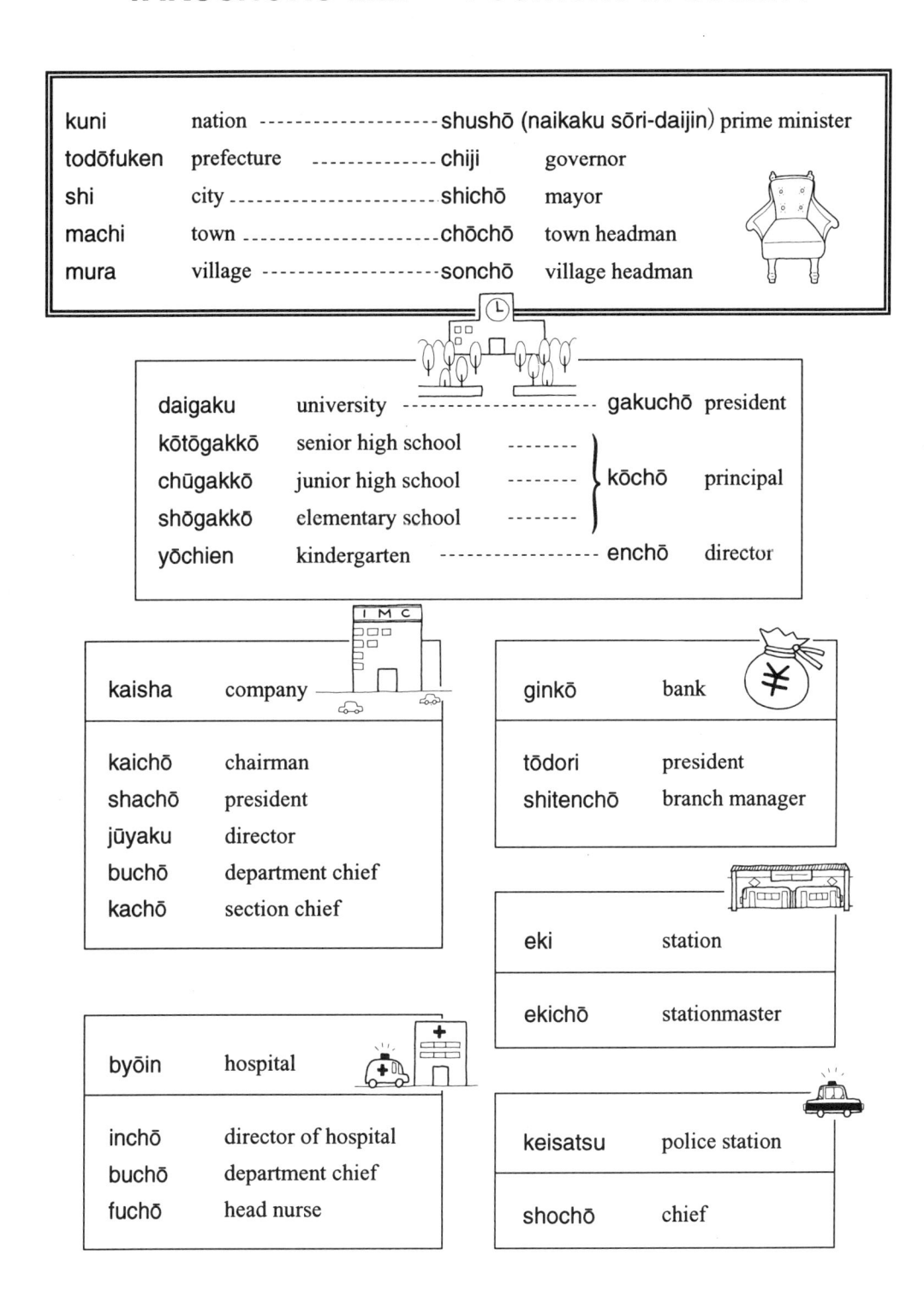

kuni	nation	shushō (naikaku sōri-daijin)	prime minister
todōfuken	prefecture	chiji	governor
shi	city	shichō	mayor
machi	town	chōchō	town headman
mura	village	sonchō	village headman

daigaku	university	gakuchō	president
kōtōgakkō	senior high school		
chūgakkō	junior high school	kōchō	principal
shōgakkō	elementary school		
yōchien	kindergarten	enchō	director

kaisha	company
kaichō	chairman
shachō	president
jūyaku	director
buchō	department chief
kachō	section chief

ginkō	bank
tōdori	president
shitenchō	branch manager

eki	station
ekichō	stationmaster

byōin	hospital
inchō	director of hospital
buchō	department chief
fuchō	head nurse

keisatsu	police station
shochō	chief

IV. Grammar Explanation

1. plain form *to omoimasu*   I think that...

   The ideas or information expressed with **omoimasu** are indicated by the particle *to*.

   1) When expressing conjecture

      ① Ashita ame ga furu to omoimasu.   I think it will rain tomorrow.
      ② Teresa-chan wa mō neta to omoimasu.
         I think Teresa has already gone to bed.

      When the content of conjecture is negative in nature, make the sentence before *to* negative.

      ③ Mirā-san wa kono nyūsu o shitte imasu ka.
         ···Iie, tabun shiranai to omoimasu.
         Does Mr. Miller know this news?
         ···No, I don't think he does.

   2) When expressing one's opinion

      ④ Nihon wa bukka ga takai to omoimasu.
         I think that prices are high in Japan.

      The expression ~*ni tsuite dō omoimasu ka* is used to ask someone's opinion on something by using **omoimasu**, *to* is not necessary after *dō*.

      ⑤ Atarashii kūkō ni tsuite dō omoimasu ka.
         ···Kirei desu ga, chotto kōtsū ga fuben da to omoimasu.
         What do you think of the new airport?
         ···I think that it is clean but the access to it is not easy.

      Agreement or disagreement with other people's opinions can be expressed as follows.

      ⑥ A : Fakusu wa benri desu ne.
         B : Watashi mo sō omoimasu.
         C : Watashi wa sō [wa] omoimasen.
         A : Fax machines are convenient, aren't they?
         B : I think so, too.
         C : I don't think so.

2. "S" / plain form *to iimasu*   say...

   The content expressed with *iimasu* is indicated by the particle *to*.

   1) When quoting directly what someone says or said, repeat exactly what they say as in the following structure.

      ⑦ Neru mae ni "Oyasuminasai" to iimasu.
         We say "Good night" before going to bed.

      ⑧ Mirā-san wa "Raishū Tōkyō e shutchō-shimasu" to iimashita.
         Mr. Miller said "I will go to Tokyo on a business trip next week."

2) When quoting indirectly what someone says or said, the plain form is used before *to*. The tense of the quoted sentence is not affected by the tense of the main sentence.

⑨ Mirā-san wa raishū Tōkyō e shutchō-suru to iimashita.
Mr. Miller said that he would go to Tokyo on a business trip next week.

3. | V / *i*-adj : plain form } *deshō?*
    | *na*-adj / N : plain form / ~*da* |

When the speaker expects that the listener has some knowledge on the topic being discussed and that the listener will agree with the speaker's view, *deshō* is said with a rising intonation to confirm the listener's agreement.

⑩ Ashita pātii ni iku deshō?
   ···Ē, ikimasu.
   You are going to the party tomorrow, aren't you?
   ···Yes, I am.

⑪ Hokkaidō wa samukatta deshō?　　　It was cold in Hokkaido, wasn't it?
   ···Iie, sonnani samukunakatta desu.　···No, it wasn't that cold.

4. | N₁ (place) *de* N₂ *ga arimasu* |

When N₂ expresses such events as a party, concert, festival, incident, disaster and so on, *arimasu* means "to take place" or "to be held."

⑫ Tōkyō de Nihon to Burajiru no sakkā no shiai ga arimasu.
   A football game between Japan and Brazil will be held in Tokyo.

5. | N (occasion) *de* |

When some action takes place on a certain occasion, that occasion is followed by *de*.

⑬ Kaigi de nanika iken o iimashita ka.
   Did you give your opinion at the meeting?

6. | N *demo* V |

demo is used to give an example out of things of the same kind (drinks in the case of ⑭) when one encourages or advises someone to do something or when one makes a suggestion.

⑭ Chotto biiru demo nomimasen ka.
   Shall we drink beer or something?

7. | V *nai*-form *nai to*······ |

This expression is made by omitting *ikemasen* from V*nai*-form *nai to ikemasen*. V*nai*-form *nai to ikemasen* is similar to V*nai*-form *nakereba narimasen* which you learned in Lesson 17.

⑮ Mō kaeranai to······.　　　　　　I have to go home now.

Lesson 22

I. Vocabulary

kimasu II [shatsu o ~]	きます [シャツを ~]	put on [a shirt, etc.]
hakimasu I [kutsu o ~]	はきます [くつを ~]	put on [shoes, trousers, etc.]
kaburimasu I [bōshi o ~]	かぶります [ぼうしを ~]	put on [a hat, etc.]
kakemasu II [megane o ~]	かけます [めがねを ~]	put on [glasses]
umaremasu II	うまれます	be born
kōto	コート	coat
sūtsu	スーツ	suit
sētā	セーター	sweater
bōshi	ぼうし	hat, cap
megane	めがね	glasses
yoku	よく	often
Omedetō gozaimasu.	おめでとう ございます。	Congratulations. (used on birthdays, at weddings, New Year's Day, etc.)

◀ Kaiwa ▶

kochira	こちら	this (polite equivalent of *kore*)
yachin	やちん	house rent
Ūn.	うーん。	Let me see.
dainingu-kichin	ダイニングキチン	kitchen with a dining area
washitsu	わしつ	Japanese-style room
oshiire	おしいれ	Japanese-style closet
futon	ふとん	Japanese-style mattress and quilt
apāto	アパート	apartment

~~~~~~~~~~~~~~~~~~~~~~~~~

Pari	パリ	Paris
Banri no chōjō	ばんりの ちょうじょう	the Great Wall of China
Yoka-kaihatsu-sentā	よかかいはつセンター	Center for Developing Leisure Activities
rejā-hakusho	レジャーはくしょ	white paper on leisure

II. Translation

Sentence Patterns

1. This is a cake Mr. Miller made.
2. That man who is over there is Mr. Miller.
3. I have forgotten the words I learned yesterday.
4. I have no time to go shopping.

Example Sentences

1. This is a photo I took on the Great Wall of China.
   ···Is it? It is superb, isn't it?
2. Which is the picture Ms. Karina drew?
   ···It is that one. That picture of the sea.
3. Who is that woman wearing the kimono?
   ···That is Ms. Kimura.
4. Mr. Yamada, where did you first meet your wife?
   ···It was Osaka Castle.
5. How was the concert you went to with Ms. Kimura?
   ···It was very good.
6. What's wrong with you?
   ···I have lost the umbrella I bought yesterday.
7. What kind of house do you want?
   ···I want a house that has a big garden.
8. Would you like to go for a drink this evening?
   ···I am sorry, but this evening I have promised to meet a friend.

Conversation

What kind of apartment would you like?

Real estate agent:	How about this one?
	The rent is 80,000 yen.
Wang:	Ummmm. It's far from the station.
Agent:	Then how about this one?
	This one's convenient. It's a three-minute walk from the station.
Wang:	Oh.
	A kitchen-dining room, a Japanese-style room, and....
	Excuse me. What is this?
Agent:	It's an "oshiire."
	It's a place to put "futon" in.
Wang:	I see.
	Can I take a look at this apartment today?
Agent:	Yes. Shall we go now?
Wang:	Yes, please.

III. Reference Words & Information

IFUKU   CLOTHES

sūtsu suit	wanpiisu one-piece dress	uwagi jacket	zubon/pantsu trousers/pants jiinzu jeans
sukāto skirt	burausu blouse	waishatsu [white] shirt	sētā sweater
mafurā muffler tebukuro gloves	shitagi underwear	kutsushita socks pansuto panty hose, tights	kimono kimono obi obi
ōbā-kōto overcoat rein-kōto raincoat	nekutai necktie beruto belt	haihiiru high heels būtsu boots undōgutsu sneakers	zōri tabi zori tabi

IV. Grammar Explanation

1. Noun modification

You learned how to modify nouns in Lesson 2 and Lesson 8.

Mirā-san no uchi	Mr. Miller's house	(L. 2)
atarashii uchi	a new house	(L. 8)
kireina uchi	a beautiful house	(L. 8)

In Japanese, whatever modifies a word, whether it's a word or a sentence, it always comes before the word to be modified. Here you learn another way to modify nouns.

2. Noun modification by sentences

1) The predicate of the sentence which modifies a noun is in the plain form.

In the case of *na*-adjective sentences, ~*da* becomes ~*na*. In the case of noun sentences ~*da* becomes ~*no*.

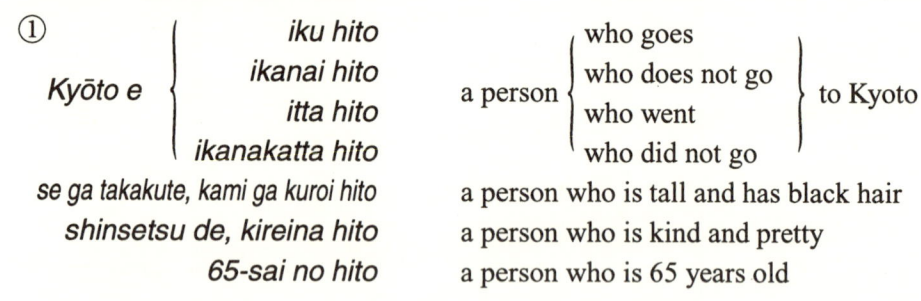

① *Kyōto e* { *iku hito* / *ikanai hito* / *itta hito* / *ikanakatta hito* } a person { who goes / who does not go / who went / who did not go } to Kyoto

se ga takakute, kami ga kuroi hito — a person who is tall and has black hair
shinsetsu de, kireina hito — a person who is kind and pretty
65-sai no hito — a person who is 65 years old

2) Nouns, which are various elements of the sentence, are picked out of it and can be modified by it.

② *Watashi wa senshū eiga o mimashita* → *Watashi ga senshū mita eiga*
  I saw a movie last week → the movie that I saw last week

③ *Wan-san wa byōin de hataraite imasu* → *Wan-san ga hataraite iru byōin*
  Mr. Wang works at a hospital → the hospital where Mr. Wang works

④ *Watashi wa ashita tomodachi ni aimasu* → *Watashi ga ashita au tomodachi*
  I will meet a friend tomorrow → the friend whom I will meet tomorrow

When the nouns underlined in ②, ③ and ④ are modified, the particles *o*, *de*, and *ni* attached to them respectively are unnecessary.

3) The noun modified by a sentence ("Mirā-san ga sunde ita uchi" in the example sentences below) can be used in various parts of a sentence.

⑤ Kore wa Mirā-san ga sunde ita uchi desu.
This is the house where Mr. Miller lived.

⑥ Mirā-san ga sunde ita uchi wa furui desu.
The house where Mr. Miller lived is old.

⑦ Mirā-san ga sunde ita uchi o kaimashita.
I bought the house where Mr. Miller lived.

⑧ Watashi wa Mirā-san ga sunde ita uchi ga suki desu.
I like the house where Mr. Miller lived.

⑨ Mirā-san ga sunde ita uchi ni neko ga imashita.
There was a cat in the house where Mr. Miller lived.

⑩ Mirā-san ga sunde ita uchi e itta koto ga arimasu.
I have been to the house where Mr. Miller lived.

3. N *ga*

When a sentence modifies a noun, the subject in the sentence is indicated by *ga*.

Mirā-san wa kēki o tsukurimashita.   Mr. Miller baked a cake.
↓

⑪ Kore wa Mirā-san ga tsukutta kēki desu.
This is the cake which Mr. Miller baked.

⑫ Watashi wa Karina-san ga kaita e ga suki desu.
I like the picture that Ms. Karina drew.

⑬ [Anata wa] kare ga umareta tokoro o shitte imasu ka.
Do you know the place where he was born?

4. V dictionary form *jikan/yakusoku/yōji*

When expressing the time for doing some activity, put the dictionary form of the action before *jikan*.

⑭ Watashi wa asagohan o taberu jikan ga arimasen.
I have no time to eat breakfast.

You can also say the content of the arrangement (appointment), etc., by putting the dictionary form of that action before *yakusoku*, etc.

⑮ Watashi wa tomodachi to eiga o miru yakusoku ga arimasu.
I have an arrangement to see a movie with a friend of mine.

⑯ Kyō wa shiyakusho e iku yōji ga arimasu.
I have something to do at the city hall today.

Lesson 23

I. Vocabulary

kikimasu I [sensei ni ~]	ききます [せんせいに ~]	ask [the teacher]
mawashimasu I	まわします	turn
hikimasu I	ひきます	pull
kaemasu II	かえます	change
sawarimasu I [doa ni ~]	さわります [ドアに ~]	touch [a door]
demasu II [otsuri ga ~]	でます [おつりが ~]	[change] come out
ugokimasu I [tokei ga ~]	うごきます [とけいが ~]	[a watch] move, work
arukimasu I [michi o ~]	あるきます [みちを ~]	walk [along a road]
watarimasu I [hashi o ~]	わたります [はしを ~]	cross [a bridge]
ki o tsukemasu II [kuruma ni ~]	きを つけます [くるまに ~]	pay attention [to cars], take care
hikkoshi-shimasu III	ひっこしします	move (house)
denki-ya	でんきや	electrician
~ ya	~や	person of ~ shop
saizu	サイズ	size
oto	おと	sound
kikai	きかい	machine
tsumami	つまみ	knob
koshō	こしょう	breakdown (~*shimasu*: break down)
michi	みち	road, way
kōsaten	こうさてん	crossroad
shingō	しんごう	traffic light
kado	かど	corner
hashi	はし	bridge
chūshajō	ちゅうしゃじょう	parking lot, car park

-me	－め	the -th (indicating order)
[o-]shōgatsu	[お]しょうがつ	New Year's Day
Gochisōsama [deshita].	ごちそうさま[でした]。	That was delicious. (said after eating or drinking)

◁ **Kaiwa** ▷

tatemono	たてもの	building
gaikokujin-tōrokushō	がいこくじんとうろくしょう	alien registration card

~~~~~~~~~~~~~~~~~~~~~~~

Shōtokutaishi	しょうとくたいし	Prince Shotoku (574 − 622)
Hōryūji	ほうりゅうじ	Horyuji Temple, a temple in Nara Prefecture built by Prince Shotoku at the beginning of the 7th century
Genki-cha	げんきちゃ	fictitious tea
Honda-eki	ほんだえき	fictitious station
Toshokan-mae	としょかんまえ	fictitious bus stop

II. Translation

Sentence Patterns
1. When you borrow books from the library, you need a card.
2. Push this button, and change will come out.

Example Sentences
1. Do you often watch TV?
   ···Well, I watch it when there is a baseball game on.
2. What do you do when there is nothing in the refrigerator?
   ···I go out and eat something at a nearby restaurant.
3. Did you turn off the air conditioner when you left the meeting room?
   ···I am sorry, I forgot.
4. Where do you buy your clothes and shoes, Mr. Santos?
   ···I buy them in my country when I go back on summer vacation or New Year vacation.
   Because the things in Japan are small for me.
5. What is that?
   ···It's "Genki-cha." I take this when I'm not in good shape.
6. Won't you come to my house when you are free?
   ···Thank you. I would love to.
7. Did you work part-time when you were a student?
   ···Yes. I sometimes did.
8. The volume is low, isn't it?
   ···Turn this knob to the right, and the volume will go up.
9. Excuse me. Where is the City Hall?
   ···Go straight down this road, and you will find it on your left.

Conversation
How can I get there?

Librarian:	Hello. This is Midori Library.
Karina:	Er, could you tell me how to get there?
Librarian:	Take a No.12 bus from Honda Station, and get off at Toshokan-mae. It's the third stop.
Karina:	The third stop, right?
Librarian:	Yes. When you get off the bus, you will see a park in front of you.
	Our library is the white building in the park.
Karina:	I see.
	Is anything required when I borrow books?
Librarian:	Are you a foreigner?
Karina:	Yes, I am.
Librarian:	Then, please bring your alien registration card.
Karina:	Yes, I will. Thank you very much.

III. Reference Words & Information

DŌRO · KŌTSŪ   ROAD & TRAFFIC

① hodō — sidewalk, pavement
② shadō — road
③ kōsoku-dōro — expressway, motorway
④ tōri — street
⑤ kōsaten — crossing
⑥ ōdan-hodō — pedestrian crossing
⑦ hodōkyō — pedestrian bridge
⑧ kado — corner
⑨ shingō — traffic light
⑩ saka — slope
⑪ fumikiri — railroad crossing
⑫ gasorin-sutando — gas station

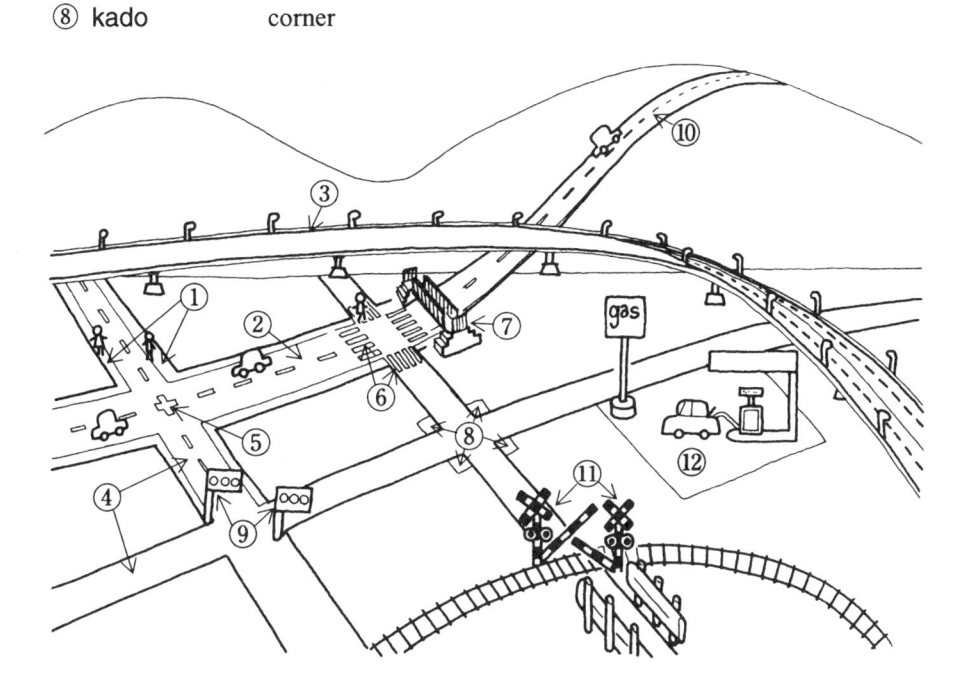

tomare	shinnyū-kinshi	ippō-tsūkō	chūsha-kinshi	usetsu-kinshi
stop	no entry	one way	no parking	no turning right

IV. Grammar Explanation

1. | V dictionary form |
   | V *nai*-form |
   | *i*-adj (~*i*) | *toki*, ~ | When..., ...
   | *na*-adj*na* |
   | N *no* |

   toki connects two sentences and expresses the time when the state or action described in the main sentence exists or occurs. As shown in the table above, the forms of verbs, *i*-adjectives, *na*-adjectives and nouns connected to *toki* are the same as the forms when modifying nouns.

   ① Toshokan de hon o kariru toki, kādo ga irimasu.
      When you borrow books from the library, you need a card.

   ② Tsukai-kata ga wakaranai toki, watashi ni kiite kudasai.
      When you don't know how to use it, ask me.

   ③ Karada no chōshi ga warui toki, "Genki-cha" o nomimasu.
      When I'm not in good shape, I drink "Genki-cha."

   ④ Himana toki, uchi e asobi ni kimasen ka.
      Won't you come to my place when you are free?

   ⑤ Tsuma ga byōki no toki, kaisha o yasumimasu.
      When my wife is sick, I take a day off work.

   ⑥ Wakai toki, amari benkyō-shimasendeshita.
      When I was young, I did not study much.

   ⑦ Kodomo no toki, yoku kawa de oyogimashita.
      I used to swim in a river when I was a child.

   The tense of adjective sentences and noun sentences which modify *toki* is not affected by the tense of the main sentence (see ⑥ and ⑦).

2. | V dictionary form | *toki*, ~
   | V *ta*-form |

   When the dictionary form of the predicate is put before *toki* it indicates the non-completion of the action, and when the *ta*-form of the predicate is put before *toki* it indicates the completion of the action.

   ⑧ Kuni e kaeru toki, kaban o kaimashita.
      I bought a bag when I went back to my country.

   ⑨ Kuni e kaetta toki, kaban o kaimashita.
      I bought a bag when I went back to my country.

   In ⑧, *kaeru* indicates that at the time being referred to the action had not been completed, that the speaker had not reached his/her country yet and that he/she bought a bag somewhere on his/her way there (Japan is included). In ⑨, *kaetta* indicates that the action was completed and the speaker bought a bag after arriving in his/her country.

3. V dictionary form *to*, ~ ..., then (inevitably)...

When expressing the situation where, as a result of a certain action, another action or matter inevitably happens, *to* is used to connect the sentences.

⑩ Kono botan o osu to, otsuri ga demasu.

Press this button, and the change will come out.

⑪ Kore o mawasu to, oto ga ōkiku narimasu.

Turn this, and the volume will go up.

⑫ Migi e magaru to, yūbinkyoku ga arimasu.

Turn to the right, and you will find the post office.

Expressions of one's will, hope, invitation or request cannot be used in the sentence which follows ~*to*.

× Jikan ga aru to,
 ┌ eiga o mi ni ikimasu. (will)
 ├ eiga o mi ni ikitai desu. (hope)
 ├ eiga o mi ni ikimasen ka. (invitation)
 └ chotto tetsudatte kudasai. (request)

In those cases, the conditional expression ~*tara* is used instead of ~*to* (see Lesson 25).

4. N *ga* adjective /V

You learned in Lesson 14 that the subject is indicated by *ga* when describing a natural phenomenon. When describing a state or a scene as it is, the subject is also indicated by *ga*.

⑬ Oto ga chiisai desu.

The volume is low.

⑭ Denki ga akaruku narimashita.

The light became brighter.

⑮ Kono botan o osu to, kippu ga demasu.

Press this button, and a ticket will come out.

5. N (place) *o* V (verb of movement)

The particle *o* is used to denote the place where a person or a thing passes. The verb of movement such as *sanpo-shimasu, watarimasu, arukimasu,*, etc. are used in this pattern.

⑯ Kōen o sanpo-shimasu.   I take a walk in the park. (L. 13)

⑰ Michi o watarimasu.   I cross the road.

⑱ Kōsaten o migi e magarimasu.   I turn to the right at the intersection.

Lesson 24

I. Vocabulary

kuremasu II	くれます	give (me)
tsurete ikimasu I	つれて いきます	take (someone)
tsurete kimasu III	つれて きます	bring (someone)
okurimasu I [hito o ～]	おくります [ひとを ～]	escort [someone], go with
shōkai-shimasu III	しょうかいします	introduce
annai-shimasu III	あんないします	show around, show the way
setsumei-shimasu III	せつめいします	explain
iremasu II [kōhii o ～]	いれます [コーヒーを ～]	make [coffee]
ojiisan/ojiichan	おじいさん/おじいちゃん	grandfather, old man
obāsan/obāchan	おばあさん/おばあちゃん	grandmother, old woman
junbi	じゅんび	preparation (～*shimasu* : prepare)
imi	いみ	meaning
[o-]kashi	[お]かし	sweets, snacks
zenbu	ぜんぶ	all
jibun de	じぶんで	by oneself

◁ Kaiwa ▷

hoka ni	ほかに	besides
wagonsha	ワゴンしゃ	station wagon
[o-]bentō	[お]べんとう	box lunch

~~~~~~~~~~~~~~~~~~~~~~~~~~~~

| Haha no hi | ははの ひ | Mother's Day |

II. Translation

Sentence Patterns
1. Ms. Sato gave me a Christmas card.
2. I lent Ms. Kimura a book.
3. I was told the telephone number of the hospital by Mr. Yamada.
4. My mother sent me a sweater.

Example Sentences
1. Do you like your grandmother, Taro?
   ···Yes, I do. She always gives me some sweets.
2. This is very delicious wine.
   ···Yes. Ms. Sato gave it to me. It's French wine.
3. Taro, what will you do for your mother on Mother's Day?
   ···I will play the piano for her.
4. Mr. Miller, did you cook all the dishes for the party yesterday by yourself?
   ···No, Mr. Wang helped me.
5. Did you go by train?
   ···No, Mr. Yamada drove me.

Conversation

Will you help me?

Karina:	Mr. Wang, you are moving house tomorrow, aren't you? Shall I come to help you?
Wang:	Thank you. Well, then, will you come around 9 o'clock?
Karina:	Who else will come to help you?
Wang:	Mr. Yamada and Mr. Miller are coming.
Karina:	What about a car?
Wang:	Mr. Yamada will lend me his station wagon.
Karina:	What about lunch?
Wang:	Well....
Karina:	Shall I bring lunch?
Wang:	Thank you. Please.
Karina:	Then see you tomorrow.

III. Reference Words & Information

ZŌTŌ NO SHŪKAN   EXCHANGE OF PRESENTS

otoshidama	small gift of money given by parents and relatives to children on New Year's Day
nyūgaku-iwai	gift celebrating admission to schools
sotsugyō-iwai	graduation gift (money, stationery, book, etc.)
kekkon-iwai	wedding gift (money, household goods, etc.)
shussan-iwai	gift celebrating a birth (baby clothes, toys, etc.)
o-chūgen [Jul. or Aug.] o-seibo [Dec.]	gift for a person whose care you are under, e.g., doctor, teacher, boss, etc. (food, etc.)
o-kōden	condolence money
o-mimai	present given when visiting a sick person (flowers, fruits, etc.)

Noshibukuro Special Envelope for Gift of Money

There are several kinds of special envelopes called NOSHIBUKURO. According to the occasion, a suitable one should be chosen.

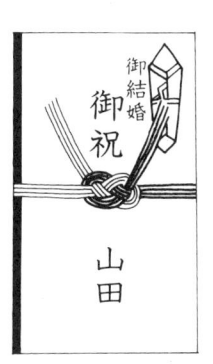

for weddings (with red and white, or gold and silver ribbon)	for celebrations other than weddings (with red and white, or gold and silver ribbon)	for funerals (with black and white ribbon)

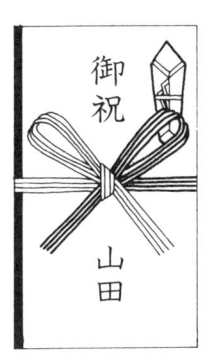

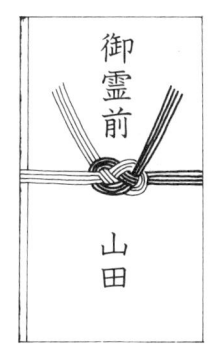

IV. Grammar Explanation

1. *kuremasu*

    You learned that *agemasu* means "give" in Lesson 7. This verb cannot be used when somebody else gives something to the speaker or the speaker's family, etc. (× *Satō-san wa watashi ni Kurisumasu-kādo o agemashita*). In this case *kuremasu* is used.

    ① Watashi wa Satō-san ni hana o agemashita.
        I gave flowers to Ms. Sato.

    ② Satō-san wa watashi ni Kurisumasu-kādo o kuremashita.
        Ms. Sato gave me a Christmas card.

    ③ Satō-san wa imōto ni o-kashi o kuremashita.
        Ms. Sato gave candies to my younger sister.

2.
    | V *te*-form | *agemasu* / *moraimasu* / *kuremasu* |

    agemasu, *moraimasu* and *kuremasu* are also used to refer to the giving and receiving of actions as well as those of things. They indicate who is doing that act for whom, while also expressing a sense of goodwill or gratitude. In this case, the act is expressed by the *te*-form.

    1) V *te*-form *agemasu*

    V *te*-form *agemasu* indicates that one does something for somebody with a sense of goodwill.

    ④ Watashi wa Kimura-san ni hon o kashite agemashita.
        I lent Ms. Kimura a book.

    When the speaker is the actor and the listener is the receiver of the act, this expression could give the impression that the speaker is being patronizing. You are, therefore, advised to avoid using this expression directly to someone whom you do not know very well or who is senior or superior to you. You may use it to someone with whom you have a very close, friendly relationship. So, when you offer assistance to someone who is not very close, V *masu*-form *mashō ka* (see Lesson 14, 6) is used.

    ⑤ Takushii o yobimashō ka.   Shall I call a taxi for you?   (L. 14)
    ⑥ Tetsudaimashō ka.   May I help you?   (L. 14)

2) V *te*-form *moraimasu*

⑦ Watashi wa Yamada-san ni toshokan no denwa-bangō o oshiete moraimashita.
Mr. Yamada told me the telephone number of the library.

This expression conveys a sense of gratitude on the part of those who receive a favor.

3) V *te*-form *kuremasu*

⑧ Haha wa [watashi ni] sētā o okutte kuremashita.
My mother sent me a sweater.

Like V *te*-form *moraimasu*, this expression also conveys a sense of gratitude on the part of those who receive a favor. The difference is that V *te*-form *moraimasu* has the receiver of the act as the subject of the sentence, while V *te*-form *kuremasu* has the actor as the subject of the sentence, implying the actor (the subject) voluntarily takes the action. The receiver of the act in the latter case is often the speaker and *watashi* (the receiver) *ni* is often omitted.

3. N(person) *ga* V

⑨ Sutekina nekutai desu ne.　　　　That's a nice tie, isn't it?
　…Ē, Satō-san ga kuremashita.　　…Yes. Ms. Sato gave it to me.

You present a topic, saying *sutekina nekutai desu ne*. Responding to it, your partner in conversation gives a piece of information on the topic which is unknown to you, [*kono nekutai wa*] *Satō-san ga kuremashita*. The subject of the sentence giving new information is indicated by *ga*.

4. Interrogative *ga* V

You learned that when the subject is questioned, it is indicated by *ga* in *arimasu / imasu* sentences (Lesson 10) and adjective sentences (Lesson 12). This is also the case for verb sentences.

⑩ Dare ga tetsudai ni ikimasu ka.　　Who will go to give him a hand?
　…Karina-san ga ikimasu.　　　　…Ms. Karina will.

Lesson 25

I. Vocabulary

kangaemasu II	かんがえます	think, consider
tsukimasu I	つきます	arrive [at the station]
[eki ni ～]	[えきに ～]	
ryūgaku-shimasu III	りゅうがくします	study abroad
torimasu I	とります	grow old
[toshi o ～]	[としを ～]	
inaka	いなか	countryside, hometown
taishikan	たいしかん	embassy
gurūpu	グループ	group
chansu	チャンス	chance
oku	おく	hundred million
moshi [～ tara]	もし [～たら]	if ～
ikura [～ te mo]	いくら [～ても]	however ～, even if ～

◁ Kaiwa ▷

tenkin	てんきん	transfer (〜shimasu : be transferred to another office)
koto	こと	thing, matter (〜no koto : thing about 〜)
Ippai nomimashō.	いっぱい のみましょう。	Let's have a drink together.
[Iroiro] osewa ni narimashita.	[いろいろ] おせわに なりました。	Thank you for everything you have done for me.
ganbarimasu I	がんばります	do one's best
Dōzo o-genki de.	どうぞ おげんきで。	Best of luck. (said when expecting a long separation)

II. Translation

Sentence Patterns
1. If it rains, I will not go out.
2. Even if it rains, I will go out.

Example Sentences
1. If you had a hundred million yen, what would you like to do?
   ···I would want to build a computer software company.
2. What will you do if your friend doesn't come at the time he promised?
   ···I will go home immediately.
3. That new shoe shop has a lot of good shoes.
   ···Does it? If their prices are reasonable, I would like to buy some.
4. Do I have to submit the report by tomorrow?
   ···No. If it's not possible, submit it on Friday.
5. Have you thought of a name for your baby yet?
   ···Yes. If it is a boy, he will be named "Hikaru," and if it is a girl, she will be named "Aya."
6. Will you start work straightaway after you graduate from university?
   ···No, I want to travel to various countries for about one year.
7. Excuse me, ma'am. But I don't understand the meaning of this word.
   ···Did you check it in the dictionary?
   Yes, I did. I still don't get it.
8. Japanese people are fond of traveling in groups, aren't they?
   ···Yes, they are, because it is economical.
   No matter how economical it is, I don't like group tours.

Conversation
Thank you for having been kind to me

Yamada:	Congratulations! You are going to be transferred.
Miller:	Thank you.
Kimura:	When you leave for Tokyo, we will miss you.
	Don't forget about Osaka after you go to Tokyo.
Miller:	Of course. Ms. Kimura, if you have time, please come to Tokyo.
Santos:	Mr. Miller, when you come to Osaka, give me a call.
	Let's have a drink.
Miller:	I'd love to.
	Thank you very much, all of you, for having been kind to me.
Sato:	Please take care of yourself and do your best.
Miller:	Yes, I will do my best. Best of luck, all of you.

III. Reference Words & Information

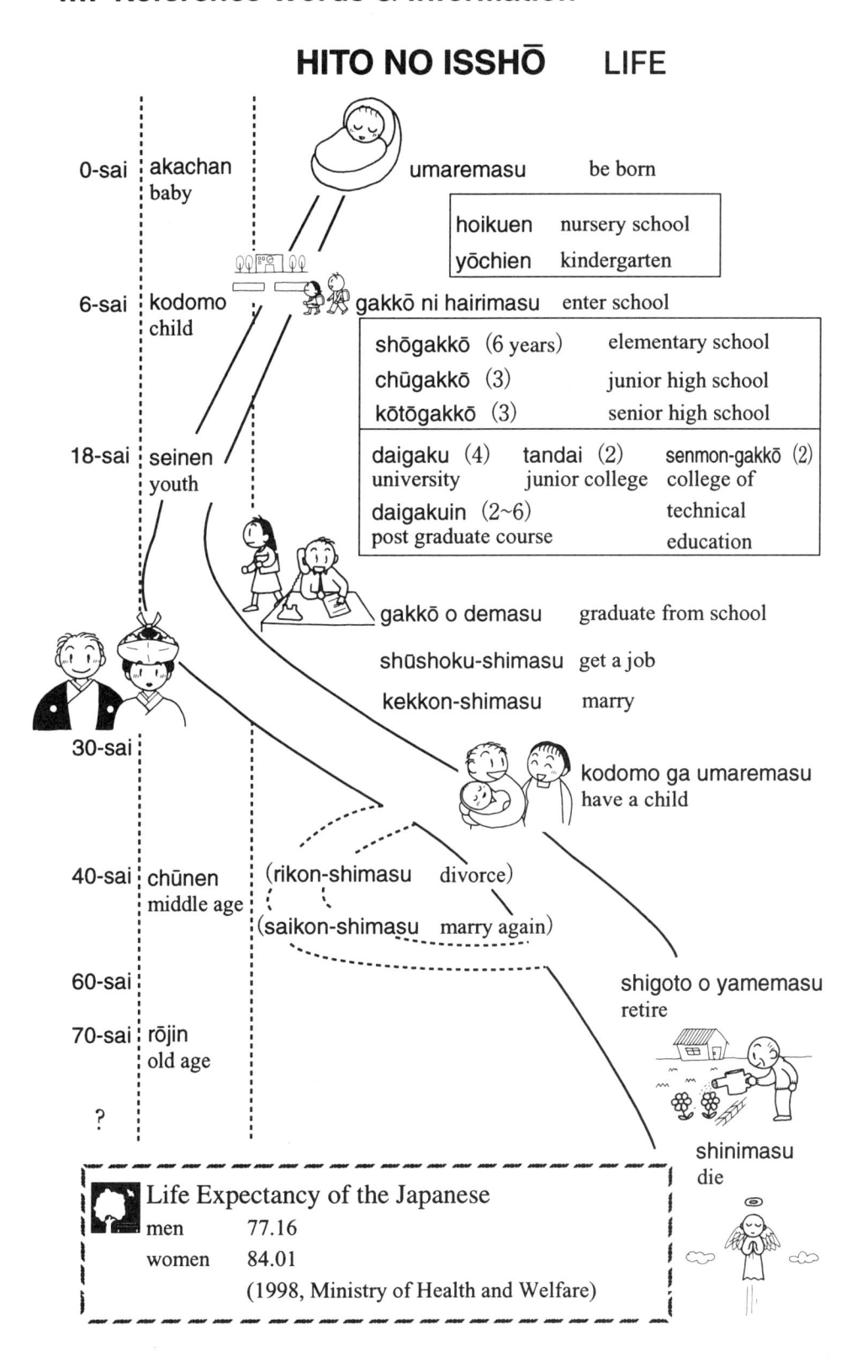

HITO NO ISSHŌ   LIFE

0-sai — akachan / baby

umaremasu — be born

| hoikuen | nursery school |
| yōchien | kindergarten |

6-sai — kodomo / child

gakkō ni hairimasu — enter school

shōgakkō (6 years)	elementary school
chūgakkō (3)	junior high school
kōtōgakkō (3)	senior high school
daigaku (4)	university
tandai (2)	junior college
senmon-gakkō (2)	college of technical education
daigakuin (2~6)	post graduate course

18-sai — seinen / youth

gakkō o demasu — graduate from school

shūshoku-shimasu — get a job

kekkon-shimasu — marry

kodomo ga umaremasu — have a child

30-sai

40-sai — chūnen / middle age

(rikon-shimasu — divorce)

(saikon-shimasu — marry again)

60-sai

shigoto o yamemasu — retire

70-sai — rōjin / old age

?

shinimasu — die

Life Expectancy of the Japanese
men   77.16
women 84.01
(1998, Ministry of Health and Welfare)

IV. Grammar Explanation

1. plain past form *ra*, ~ If...

   When *ra* is attached to the past tense plain form of verbs, adjectives, etc., it changes the preceding clause into a conditional expression. When a speaker wants to state his opinion, situation, request, etc., in the conditional, this pattern is used.

   ① Okane ga attara, ryokō-shimasu.
      If I had money, I would travel.

   ② Jikan ga nakattara, terebi o mimasen.
      If I don't have time, I will not watch TV.

   ③ Yasukattara, pasokon o kaitai desu.
      If it's inexpensive, I want to buy a personal computer.

   ④ Hima dattara, tetsudatte kudasai.
      If you are free, please give me a hand.

   ⑤ Ii tenki dattara, sanpo-shimasen ka.
      If it's fine, won't you take a walk with me?

2. V *ta*-form *ra*, ~ When.../After...

   This pattern is used to express that a certain action will be done or a certain situation will appear when a matter, action or state which is sure to happen in the future has been completed or achieved. The main sentence is always in the present tense.

   ⑥ 10-ji ni nattara, dekakemashō.
      Let's go out when it gets to ten.

   ⑦ Uchi e kaettara, sugu shawā o abimasu.
      I take a shower soon after I return home.

3.
V *te*-form	
i-adj (~*i̶*)	→~*kute*
na-adj [*n̶a̶*]	→*de*
N *de*	

   mo, ~ Even if...

   This expression is used to present a reverse condition. Contrary to plain past form *ra*, ~, this expression is used when an action which is expected to be taken or an event which is expected to happen naturally under the given circumstances does not materialize or a thing turns out in a way opposite to a socially accepted idea.

⑧ Ame ga futte mo, sentaku-shimasu.
　　Even if it rains, I'll do the laundry.

⑨ Yasukute mo, watashi wa gurūpu-ryokō ga kirai desu.
　　Even if group tours are inexpensive, I don't like them.

⑩ Benri de mo, pasokon o tsukaimasen.
　　Even if a personal computer is useful, I won't use it.

⑪ Nichi-yōbi de mo, hatarakimasu.
　　Even if it is Sunday, I will work.

4. *moshi* and *ikura*

moshi is used in a sentence in the plain past form to indicate beforehand that the sentence is going to present a condition, while *ikura* is used with ～*te mo* (～*de mo*) to do the same. *moshi* implies that an emphasis is on the speaker's supposition while *ikura* is meant to stress the degree of conditionality.

⑫ Moshi 1-oku-en attara, iroirona kuni o ryokō-shitai desu.
　　If I had 100 million yen, I would want to travel in various countries.

⑬ Ikura kangaete mo, wakarimasen.
　　No matter how much I think, I can't understand this.

⑭ Ikura takakute mo, kaimasu.
　　No matter how expensive it is, I will buy it.

5. N *ga*

As mentioned in Lesson 16, 4. [Note], the subject of a subordinate clause is indicated by *ga*. In subordinate clauses using *tara*, *te mo*, *toki*, *to*, *mae ni*, etc., in addition to *kara*, the subject is indicated by *ga*, as shown below.

⑮ Tomodachi ga kuru mae ni, heya o sōji-shimasu.
　　I will clean my room before my friends come.　　　　　　　　(L. 18)

⑯ Tsuma ga byōki no toki, kaisha o yasumimasu.
　　When my wife is sick, I take a day off work.　　　　　　　　　(L. 23)

⑰ Tomodachi ga yakusoku no jikan ni konakattara, dō shimasu ka.
　　If your friend doesn't come on time, what will you do?　　　　(L. 25)

SUMMARY LESSON

I. Particles

1. [wa]
- A: 1) I am Mike Miller. (Lesson 1)
-    2) I get up at six in the morning. (4)
-    3) Cherry blossoms are beautiful. (8)
- B: 1) What time is it now in New York? (4)
-    2) On Sunday I went to Nara with a friend. (6)
-    3) Tokyo Disneyland is in Chiba Prefecture. (10)
-    4) Please send the data by fax. (17)

2. [mo]
- A: 1) Maria is Brazilian, too. (1)
-    2) Please send this parcel, too. (11)
-    3) I like both. (12)
-    4) I have been on a diet many times. (19)
- B: 1) I did not go anywhere. (5)
-    2) I did not eat anything. (6)
-    3) There was no one. (10)

3. [no]
- A: 1) That person is Mr. Miller of IMC. (1)
-    2) This is a book on computers. (2)
-    3) That is my umbrella. (2)
-    4) This is a Japanese car. (3)
-    5) Did you study last night? (4)
-    6) How are your Japanese studies going? (8)
-    7) There is a picture on the desk. (10)
-    8) Please tell me how to read this Kanji. (14)
-    9) I came from Bandung, Indonesia. (16)
- B: 1) This bag is Ms. Sato's. (2)
-    2) Where was this camera made?
      ···In Japan. (3)
- C: Is there one a little bigger? (14)

4. [o]
- A: 1) I drink juice. (6)
-    2) I am going to travel for a week. (11)
-    3) I will pick up my child at two o'clock. (13)

B: 1) I took a day off work yesterday. (11)
    2) I leave home at eight every morning. (13)
    3) I get off the train at Kyoto. (16)
C: 1) I take a walk in a park every morning. (13)
    2) Please cross at that traffic signal. (23)
    3) Go straight along this street and you will find the station. (23)

5. [ga]

A: 1) I like Italian food. (9)
    2) Mr. Miller is good at cooking. (9)
    3) I understand Japanese a little. (9)
    4) Do you have any small change? (9)
    5) I have two children. (11)
    6) I want a personal computer. (13)
    7) Can you ski? (18)
    8) I need a tape recorder. (20)
B: 1) There is a man over there. (10)
    2) There is a picture on the desk. (10)
    3) There will be a festival in Kyoto next month. (21)
C: 1) Tokyo has a big population. (12)
    2) Mr. Santos is tall. (16)
    3) I have a sore throat. (17)
D: 1) Which is faster, a bus or a train?
        …A train is faster. (12)
    2) Baseball is the most interesting of all the sports. (12)
E: 1) It is raining now. (14)
    2) Touch this, and the water will come out. (23)
    3) The volume is low. (23)
F: 1) I am going to go and have a meal after the concert is over. (16)
    2) What will you do if your friend does not come on time? (25)
    3) When my wife is sick, I take a day off work. (23)
    4) Which is the picture that Ms. Karina drew? (22)
G: 1) Ms. Sato gave me wine. (24)
    2) Who paid for you? (24)

6. [ni]

A: 1) I get up at six o'clock in the morning. (4)
    2) I came to Japan on March 25th. (5)
B: 1) I gave some flowers to Ms. Kimura. (7)
    2) I write Christmas cards to my family and friends. (7)

C:	1)	I received a gift from Mr. Santos.	(7)
	2)	I borrowed a book from a person in the company.	(7)
D:	1)	There is a picture on the desk.	(10)
	2)	My family is in New York.	(10)
	3)	Maria lives in Osaka.	(15)
E:	1)	I will meet a friend tomorrow.	(6)
	2)	Have you already got accustomed to living in Japan?	(8)
	3)	Let's go in that coffee shop.	(13)
	4)	Please sit here.	(15)
	5)	I take a train from Umeda.	(16)
	6)	Please write your name here.	(14)
	7)	Touch this, and the water will come out.	(23)
F:		I play tennis once a week.	(11)
G:	1)	I came to Japan to study economics.	(13)
	2)	I will go to Kyoto for cherry blossom viewing.	(13)
H:		Teresa became ten.	(19)

7. [e]

1)	I will go to Kyoto with a friend.	(5)
2)	I will go to France to study cooking.	(13)
3)	Please turn right at that traffic light.	(14)

8. [de]

A:	1)	I go home by taxi.	(5)
	2)	I send the data by fax.	(7)
	3)	Do you write reports in Japanese?	(7)
B:	1)	I buy a newspaper at the station.	(6)
	2)	In July there is a festival in Kyoto.	(21)
C:		I like summer the best of the year.	(12)

9. [to]

A:	1)	I came to Japan with my family.	(5)
	2)	Ms. Sato is talking with the department chief in the meeting room.	(14)
B:	1)	I have Saturdays and Sundays off.	(4)
	2)	The book store is between a florist's and a supermarket.	(10)
	3)	Which is more interesting, football or baseball?	(12)
C:	1)	I think it will rain tomorrow.	(21)
	2)	The prime minister said that he would go to America next month.	(21)

10. [ya]

There are old letters, pictures and things in the box.	(10)

11. [kara] [made]
A: 1) I work from nine to five. (4)
2) The bank is open from nine to three. (4)
3) I worked until ten last night. (4)
B: 1) Chili sauce is on the second rack from the bottom. (10)
2) It takes four hours to fly from my country to Japan. (11)
3) Shall I come and get you at the station? (14)

12. [made ni]
I have to return the books by Saturday. (17)

13. [yori]
China is bigger than Japan. (12)

14. [demo]
Shall we drink a glass of beer or something? (21)

15. [ka]
A: 1) Is Mr. Santos Brazilian? (1)
2) Is it a mechanical pencil or a ballpoint pen? (2)
3) Shall we go and see a film together? (6)
B: Excuse me. Where is Yunyu-ya store?
⋯Yunyu-ya store? It's in that building. (10)
C: Is this umbrella yours?
⋯No, it isn't. It's Mr. Schmidt's.
I see. (2)

16. [ne]
1) I studied until twelve last night, too.
⋯That's tough, isn't it? (4)
2) That spoon looks nice, doesn't it? (7)
3) Well,⋯let me see, it's 871-6813.
⋯871-6813, right? (4)
4) You see the man over there. Who is he? (10)

17. [yo]
Does this train go to Koshien?
⋯No. The next local train does. (5)

II. How to Use the Forms

1. [masu-form]

masu-form masen ka	Won't you have some tea with me?	(Lesson 6)
masu-form mashō	Let's meet at five.	(6)
masu-form tai desu	I want to buy a camera.	(13)
masu-form ni ikimasu	I go to see a movie.	(13)
masu-form mashō ka	Shall I call a taxi for you?	(14)

2. [te-form]

te-form kudasai	Please lend me your ballpoint pen.	(14)
te-form imasu	Ms. Sato is now talking with Mr. Miller.	(14)
	Maria lives in Osaka.	(15)
te-form mo ii desu	May I smoke?	(15)
te-form wa ikemasen	Don't take photographs in the museum.	(15)
te-form kara, ~	After I finish work, I go swimming.	(16)
te-form, te-form, ~	In the morning, I go jogging, take a shower, then go to the office.	(16)
te-form agemasu	I lend a CD to Mr. Miller.	(24)
te-form moraimasu	Ms. Sato took me to Osaka Castle.	(24)
te-form kuremasu	Mr. Yamada took me in his car.	(24)

3. [nai-form]

nai-form nai de kudasai	Please do not take photographs here.	(17)
nai-form nakereba narimasen	You must show your passport.	(17)
nai-form nakute mo ii desu	You don't need to take off your shoes.	(17)

4. [dictionary form]

dictionary form koto ga dekimasu	I can play the piano.	(18)
dictionary form koto desu	My hobby is watching movies.	(18)
dictionary form mae ni, ~	I read a book before going to bed.	(18)
dictionary form to, ~	Turn to the right, and you'll find a post office.	(23)

5. [ta-form]

ta-form koto ga arimasu	I have been to Hokkaido.	(19)
ta-form ri, ta-form ri shimasu	On my holidays I play tennis, take walks and so forth.	(19)

6. [plain form]
   plain form to omoimasu

I think that Mr. Miller has already gone home.	(21)
I think that things are expensive in Japan.	(21)
I think that family is the most important thing.	(21)

   plain form to iimasu — My brother said that he would return by ten. (21)

   verb ⎫
   i-adjective ⎬ plain form ⎫
   na-adjective ⎬ plain form ⎬ deshō?
   noun ⎭ ~dá ⎭

Tomorrow you will go to the party, won't you?	(21)
The morning rush hours are terrible, aren't they?	(21)
Personal computers are useful, aren't they?	(21)
He is American, isn't he?	(21)

   verb plain form noun — This is the cake that I made. (22)

7. verb plain form ⎫
   i-adjective ⎬ toki, ~
   na-adjective na ⎬
   noun no ⎭

When I read a paper, I put on my glasses.	(23)
When I am sleepy, I drink coffee.	(23)
When I have time, I watch video tapes.	(23)
When it rains, I take a taxi.	(23)

8. plain form past ra, ~

If I have a personal computer, it'll be convenient.	(25)
If the personal computer is cheap, I will buy it.	(25)
If it's simple to use, I will buy it.	(25)
If it's fine, I'll take a walk.	(25)

9. verb te-form ⎫
   i-adjective ~kute ⎬ mo, ~
   na-adjective de ⎬
   noun de ⎭

Though I've checked in the dictionary, I don't understand its meaning.	(25)
Even if personal computers are cheap, I won't buy one.	(25)
Even if you don't like it, you should eat it.	(25)
He works even on Sundays.	(25)

III. Adverbs and Adverbial Expressions

1. minna — The foreign teachers are all Americans. (Lesson 11)
　　zenbu — I have finished all my homework. (24)
　　takusan — I have a lot of work. (9)
　　totemo — It is very cold in Beijing. (8)
　　yoku — Mr. Wang understands English well. (9)
　　daitai — Teresa understands most Hiragana. (9)
　　sukoshi — Maria understands Katakana a little. (9)
　　chotto — Let's take a rest for a while. (6)
　　mō sukoshi — Don't you have one a little bit smaller? (14)
　　mō — Make one more copy, please. (14)
　　zutto — There are a lot more people in Tokyo than in New York. (12)
　　ichiban — I like tempura best of all Japanese dishes. (12)
　　　　— Notebooks are on the top of that shelf. (10)

2. itsumo — I always have lunch in the university dining hall. (6)
　　tokidoki — I sometimes eat at a restaurant. (6)
　　yoku — Mr. Miller often goes to coffee shops. (22)
　　hajimete — Yesterday I ate sushi for the first time. (12)
　　mata — Please come again tomorrow. (14)
　　mō ichido — Once again, please. (II)

3. ima — It is now ten past two. (4)
　　sugu — Please send the report at once. (14)
　　mō — I have already bought my Shinkansen ticket. (7)
　　　　— It's eight o'clock now, isn't it? (8)
　　mada — Have you had lunch?
　　　　　　···No, not yet. (7)
　　korekara — I'm going to take lunch from now. (7)
　　sorosoro — It is almost time for me to leave. (8)
　　ato de — I will come later. (14)
　　mazu — First, push this button. (16)
　　tsugi ni — Next, insert the card. (16)
　　saikin — Recently Japanese football teams have become stronger. (21)

4. jibun de — I cooked all the dishes for the party by myself. (24)
　　hitori de — I go to the hospital alone. (5)
　　minna de — We will go to Kyoto all together tomorrow. (20)
　　issho ni — Won't you drink some beer with me? (6)
　　betsubetsu ni — Please charge us separately. (13)
　　zenbu de — It is five hundred yen in all. (11)

hoka ni	Who will come to help you other than me?	(24)
hayaku	I'll go home early.	(9)
yukkuri	Please speak slowly.	(14)
	Have a good rest, today.	(17)
dandan	It will get hotter and hotter from now on.	(19)
massugu	Please go straight.	(14)
5. amari	That dictionary is not very good.	(8)
zenzen	I don't understand Indonesian at all.	(9)
nakanaka	You can hardly ever see horses in Japan.	(18)
ichido mo	I have never eaten sushi.	(19)
zehi	I am eager to go to Hokkaido.	(18)
tabun	I think Mr. Miller probably doesn't know.	(21)
kitto	I am sure it will be fine tomorrow.	(21)
moshi	If I had one hundred million yen, I would like to form my own company.	(25)
ikura	However cheap group tours are, I don't like them.	(25)
6. tokuni	In that film, the father, especially, acted well.	(15)
jitsuwa	I am on a diet actually.	(19)
hontō ni	I think food really costs a lot in Japan.	(21)
mochiron	I think Brazil will win the game, of course.	(21)

IV. Various Conjunctions

1. soshite   Subways in Tokyo are clean and convenient.   (Lesson 8)
     ～ de   Nara is a quiet and beautiful city.   (16)
     ～ kute   This personal computer is light and handy.   (16)
     sorekara   Send this by special delivery, please. And this parcel, too.   (11)
     ～ tari   On holidays I play tennis, go on walks and so on.   (19)
     ～ ga   Excuse me, but lend me a ballpoint pen, please.   (14)

2. sorekara   I studied Japanese, and then saw a movie.   (6)
     ～ te kara   We dined at a restaurant after the concert was over.   (16)
     ～ te, ～ te   In the morning I jog, take a shower, and go to the office.   (16)
     ～ mae ni   I write in my diary before going to bed.   (18)
     ～ toki   When you borrow books from the library, you need a card.   (23)

3. kara   I don't go anywhere, because I don't have the time.   (9)
     desukara   Today is my wife's birthday. So I must go home early.   (17)

4. ～ ga   'The Seven Samurai' is an old but interesting movie.   (8)
     demo   The tour was fun. But I got tired.   (12)
     ～ kedo   This curry is hot but tasty.   (20)
     shikashi   Dancing is good for the health, so I will practice it every day from tomorrow.
          ···But excessive practice is not good for one's health.   (19)

5. ja   This is an Italian wine.
          ···Well, I'll buy it.   (3)
     ～ to   Push this button, and change will come out.   (23)
     ～ tara   If it rains, I will not go out.   (25)

6. ～ te mo   Even if it rains, I will go out.   (25)

APPENDICES

I. Numerals

0	zero, rei	100	hyaku
1	ichi	200	ni-hyaku
2	ni	300	san-byaku
3	san	400	yon-hyaku
4	yon, shi	500	go-hyaku
5	go	600	rop-pyaku
6	roku	700	nana-hyaku
7	nana, shichi	800	hap-pyaku
8	hachi	900	kyū-hyaku
9	kyū, ku		
10	jū	1,000	sen
11	jū-ichi	2,000	ni-sen
12	jū-ni	3,000	san-zen
13	jū-san	4,000	yon-sen
14	jū-yon, jū-shi	5,000	go-sen
15	jū-go	6,000	roku-sen
16	jū-roku	7,000	nana-sen
17	jū-nana, jū-shichi	8,000	has-sen
18	jū-hachi	9,000	kyū-sen
19	jū-kyū, jū-ku		
20	ni-jū	10,000	ichi-man
30	san-jū	100,000	jū-man
40	yon-jū	1,000,000	hyaku-man
50	go-jū	10,000,000	sen-man
60	roku-jū	100,000,000	ichi-oku
70	nana-jū, shichi-jū		
80	hachi-jū	17.5	jū-nana ten go
90	kyū-jū	0.83	rei ten hachi san
		$\frac{1}{2}$	ni-bun no ichi
		$\frac{3}{4}$	yon-bun no san

II. Expressions of time

day	morning	night
ototoi the day before yesterday	ototoi no asa the morning before last	ototoi no ban the night before last
kinō yesterday	kinō no asa yesterday morning	kinō no ban last night
kyō today	kesa this morning	konban tonight
ashita tomorrow	ashita no asa tomorrow morning	ashita no ban tomorrow night
asatte the day after tomorrow	asatte no asa the morning after next	asatte no ban the night after next
mainichi every day	maiasa every morning	maiban every night

shi - assatte

week	month	year
sensenshū (ni-shūkan mae) the week before last	sensengetsu (ni-kagetsu mae) the month before last	ototoshi the year before last
senshū last week	sengetsu last month	kyonen last year
konshū this week	kongetsu this month	kotoshi this year
raishū next week	raigetsu next month	rainen next year
saraishū the week after next	saraigetsu the month after next	sarainen the year after next
maishū every week	maitsuki every month	maitoshi, mainen every year

Telling time

	o'clock -ji		minute -fun/-pun
1	ichi-ji	1	ip-pun
2	ni-ji	2	ni-fun
3	san-ji	3	san-pun
4	yo-ji	4	yon-pun
5	go-ji	5	go-fun
6	roku-ji	6	rop-pun
7	shichi-ji	7	nana-fun, shichi-fun
8	hachi-ji	8	hap-pun
9	ku-ji	9	kyū-fun
10	jū-ji	10	jup-pun, jip-pun
11	jū ichi-ji	15	jū go-fun
12	jū ni-ji	30	san-jup-pun, san-jip-pun, han
?	nan-ji	?	nan-pun

the days of the week -yōbi

nichi-yōbi	Sunday
getsu-yōbi	Monday
ka-yōbi	Tuesday
sui-yōbi	Wednesday
moku-yōbi	Thursday
kin-yōbi	Friday
do-yōbi	Saturday
nan-yōbi	what day

date

	month -gatsu		day -nichi		
1	ichi-gatsu	1	tsuitachi	17	jū shichi-nichi
2	ni-gatsu	2	futsuka	18	jū hachi-nichi
3	san-gatsu	3	mikka	19	jū ku-nichi
4	shi-gatsu	4	yokka	20	hatsuka
5	go-gatsu	5	itsuka	21	ni-jū ichi-nichi
6	roku-gatsu	6	muika	22	ni-jū ni-nichi
7	shichi-gatsu	7	nanoka	23	ni-jū san-nichi
8	hachi-gatsu	8	yōka	24	ni-jū yokka
9	ku-gatsu	9	kokonoka	25	ni-jū go-nichi
10	jū-gatsu	10	tōka	26	ni-jū roku-nichi
11	jū ichi-gatsu	11	jū ichi-nichi	27	ni-jū shichi-nichi
12	jū ni-gatsu	12	jū ni-nichi	28	ni-jū hachi-nichi
?	nan-gatsu	13	jū san-nichi	29	ni-jū ku-nichi
		14	jū yokka	30	san-jū-nichi
		15	jū go-nichi	31	san-jū ichi-nichi
		16	jū roku-nichi	?	nan-nichi

III. Expressions of period

	time duration	
	hour -jikan	**minute** -fun/-pun
1	ichi-jikan	ip-pun
2	ni-jikan	ni-fun
3	san-jikan	san-pun
4	yo-jikan	yon-pun
5	go-jikan	go-fun
6	roku-jikan	rop-pun
7	nana-jikan, shichi-jikan	nana-fun, shichi-fun
8	hachi-jikan	hap-pun
9	ku-jikan	kyū-fun
10	jū-jikan	jup-pun, jip-pun
?	nan-jikan	nan-pun

	period			
	day -nichi	**week** -shūkan	**month** -kagetsu	**year** -nen
1	ichi-nichi	is-shūkan	ik-kagetsu	ichi-nen
2	futsuka	ni-shūkan	ni-kagetsu	ni-nen
3	mikka	san-shūkan	san-kagetsu	san-nen
4	yokka	yon-shūkan	yon-kagetsu	yo-nen
5	itsuka	go-shūkan	go-kagetsu	go-nen
6	muika	roku-shūkan	rok-kagetsu, hantoshi	roku-nen
7	nanoka	nana-shūkan, shichi-shūkan	nana-kagetsu, shichi-kagetsu	nana-nen, shichi-nen
8	yōka	has-shūkan	hachi-kagetsu, hak-kagetsu	hachi-nen
9	kokonoka	kyū-shūkan	kyū-kagetsu	kyū-nen
10	tōka	jus-shūkan, jis-shūkan	juk-kagetsu, jik-kagetsu	jū-nen
?	nan-nichi	nan-shūkan	nan-kagetsu	nan-nen

IV. Counters

	things	persons	order	thin & flat things
		-nin	-ban	-mai
1	hitotsu	hitori	ichi-ban	ichi-mai
2	futatsu	futari	ni-ban	ni-mai
3	mittsu	san-nin	san-ban	san-mai
4	yottsu	yo-nin	yon-ban	yon-mai
5	itsutsu	go-nin	go-ban	go-mai
6	muttsu	roku-nin	roku-ban	roku-mai
7	nanatsu	nana-nin, shichi-nin	nana-ban	nana-mai
8	yattsu	hachi-nin	hachi-ban	hachi-mai
9	kokonotsu	kyū-nin	kyū-ban	kyū-mai
10	tō	jū-nin	jū-ban	jū-mai
?	ikutsu	nan-nin	nan-ban	nan-mai

	machines & vehicles	age	books & notebooks	clothes
	-dai	-sai	-satsu	-chaku
1	ichi-dai	is-sai	is-satsu	it-chaku
2	ni-dai	ni-sai	ni-satsu	ni-chaku
3	san-dai	san-sai	san-satsu	san-chaku
4	yon-dai	yon-sai	yon-satsu	yon-chaku
5	go-dai	go-sai	go-satsu	go-chaku
6	roku-dai	roku-sai	roku-satsu	roku-chaku
7	nana-dai	nana-sai	nana-satsu	nana-chaku
8	hachi-dai	has-sai	has-satsu	hat-chaku
9	kyū-dai	kyū-sai	kyū-satsu	kyū-chaku
10	jū-dai	jus-sai, jis-sai	jus-satsu, jis-satsu	jut-chaku, jit-chaku
?	nan-dai	nan-sai	nan-satsu	nan-chaku

	frequency	small things	shoes & socks	houses
	-kai	-ko	-soku/-zoku	-ken/-gen
1	ik-kai	ik-ko	is-soku	ik-ken
2	ni-kai	ni-ko	ni-soku	ni-ken
3	san-kai	san-ko	san-zoku	san-gen
4	yon-kai	yon-ko	yon-soku	yon-ken
5	go-kai	go-ko	go-soku	go-ken
6	rok-kai	rok-ko	roku-soku	rok-ken
7	nana-kai	nana-ko	nana-soku	nana-ken
8	hak-kai	hak-ko	has-soku	hak-ken
9	kyū-kai	kyū-ko	kyū-soku	kyū-ken
10	juk-kai, jik-kai	juk-ko, jik-ko	jus-soku, jis-soku	juk-ken, jik-ken
?	nan-kai	nan-ko	nan-zoku	nan-gen

	floors of a building	thin & long things	drinks & so on in cups & glasses	small animals, fish & insects
	-kai/-gai	-hon/-pon/-bon	-hai/-pai/-bai	-hiki/-piki/-biki
1	ik-kai	ip-pon	ip-pai	ip-piki
2	ni-kai	ni-hon	ni-hai	ni-hiki
3	san-gai	san-bon	san-bai	san-biki
4	yon-kai	yon-hon	yon-hai	yon-hiki
5	go-kai	go-hon	go-hai	go-hiki
6	rok-kai	rop-pon	rop-pai	rop-piki
7	nana-kai	nana-hon	nana-hai	nana-hiki
8	hak-kai	hap-pon	hap-pai	hap-piki
9	kyū-kai	kyū-hon	kyū-hai	kyū-hiki
10	juk-kai, jik-kai	jup-pon, jip-pon	jup-pai, jip-pai	jup-piki, jip-piki
?	nan-gai	nan-bon	nan-bai	nan-biki

V. Conjugation of verbs

I−group

	masu-form	te-form	dictionary form
aimasu [tomodachi ni ~]	ai masu	atte	au
araimasu	arai masu	aratte	arau
arimasu	ari masu	atte	aru
arimasu	ari masu	atte	aru
arimasu [o-matsuri ga ~]	ari masu	atte	aru
arukimasu [michi o ~]	aruki masu	aruite	aruku
asobimasu	asobi masu	asonde	asobu
dashimasu [tegami o ~]	dashi masu	dashite	dasu
dashimasu	dashi masu	dashite	dasu
dashimasu [repōto o ~]	dashi masu	dashite	dasu
furimasu [ame ga ~]	furi masu	futte	furu
hairimasu [kissaten ni ~]	hairi masu	haitte	hairu
hairimasu [daigaku ni ~]	hairi masu	haitte	hairu
hairimasu [o-furo ni ~]	hairi masu	haitte	hairu
hakimasu [kutsu o ~]	haki masu	haite	haku
hanashimasu	hanashi masu	hanashite	hanasu
haraimasu	harai masu	haratte	harau
hatarakimasu	hataraki masu	hataraite	hataraku
hikimasu	hiki masu	hiite	hiku
hikimasu	hiki masu	hiite	hiku
iimasu	ii masu	itte	iu
ikimasu	iki masu	itte	iku
irimasu [biza ga ~]	iri masu	itte	iru
isogimasu	isogi masu	isoide	isogu
kaburimasu [bōshi o ~]	kaburi masu	kabutte	kaburu
kachimasu	kachi masu	katte	katsu
kaeshimasu	kaeshi masu	kaeshite	kaesu
kaerimasu	kaeri masu	kaette	kaeru
kaimasu	kai masu	katte	kau
kakarimasu	kakari masu	kakatte	kakaru

nai-form		ta-form	meaning	lesson
awa	nai	atta	meet [a friend]	6
arawa	nai	aratta	wash	18
—	nai	atta	have	9
—	nai	atta	exist, be (inanimate things)	10
—	nai	atta	[a festival] be held, take place	21
aruka	nai	aruita	walk [along a road]	23
asoba	nai	asonda	enjoy oneself, play	13
dasa	nai	dashita	send [a letter]	13
dasa	nai	dashita	take out, withdraw	16
dasa	nai	dashita	hand in [a report]	17
fura	nai	futta	rain	14
haira	nai	haitta	enter [a coffee shop]	13
haira	nai	haitta	enter [university]	16
haira	nai	haitta	take [a bath]	17
haka	nai	haita	put on [shoes, trousers, etc.]	22
hanasa	nai	hanashita	speak, talk	14
harawa	nai	haratta	pay	17
hataraka	nai	hataraita	work	4
hika	nai	hiita	play (stringed instrument or piano, etc.)	18
hika	nai	hiita	pull	23
iwa	nai	itta	say	21
ika	nai	itta	go	5
ira	nai	itta	need, require [a visa]	20
isoga	nai	isoida	hurry	14
kabura	nai	kabutta	put on [a hat, etc.]	22
kata	nai	katta	win	21
kaesa	nai	kaeshita	give back, return	17
kaera	nai	kaetta	go home, return	5
kawa	nai	katta	buy	6
kakara	nai	kakatta	take (referring to time or money)	11

	masu-form		te-form	dictionary form
kakimasu	kaki	masu	kaite	kaku
kashimasu	kashi	masu	kashite	kasu
keshimasu	keshi	masu	keshite	kesu
kikimasu	kiki	masu	kiite	kiku
kikimasu [sensei ni ~]	kiki	masu	kiite	kiku
kirimasu	kiri	masu	kitte	kiru
machimasu	machi	masu	matte	matsu
magarimasu [migi e ~]	magari	masu	magatte	magaru
mawashimasu	mawashi	masu	mawashite	mawasu
mochimasu	mochi	masu	motte	motsu
moraimasu	morai	masu	moratte	morau
motte ikimasu	motte iki	masu	motte itte	motte iku
nakushimasu	nakushi	masu	nakushite	nakusu
naoshimasu	naoshi	masu	naoshite	naosu
naraimasu	narai	masu	naratte	narau
narimasu	nari	masu	natte	naru
noborimasu [yama ni ~]	nobori	masu	nobotte	noboru
nomimasu	nomi	masu	nonde	nomu
nomimasu [kusuri o ~]	nomi	masu	nonde	nomu
norimasu [densha ni ~]	nori	masu	notte	noru
nugimasu	nugi	masu	nuide	nugu
okimasu	oki	masu	oite	oku
okurimasu	okuri	masu	okutte	okuru
okurimasu [hito o ~]	okuri	masu	okutte	okuru
omoimasu	omoi	masu	omotte	omou
omoidashimasu	omoidashi	masu	omoidashite	omoidasu
oshimasu	oshi	masu	oshite	osu
owarimasu	owari	masu	owatte	owaru
oyogimasu	oyogi	masu	oyoide	oyogu
sawarimasu [doa ni ~]	sawari	masu	sawatte	sawaru

nai-form		ta-form	meaning	lesson
kaka	nai	kaita	write, draw, paint	6
kasa	nai	kashita	lend	7
kesa	nai	keshita	turn off	14
kika	nai	kiita	hear, listen	6
kika	nai	kiita	ask [a teacher]	23
kira	nai	kitta	cut, slice	7
mata	nai	matta	wait	14
magara	nai	magatta	turn [to the right]	14
mawasa	nai	mawashita	turn	23
mota	nai	motta	hold	14
morawa	nai	moratta	receive	7
motte ika	nai	motte itta	take (something)	17
nakusa	nai	nakushita	lose	17
naosa	nai	naoshita	repair, correct	20
narawa	nai	naratta	learn	7
nara	nai	natta	become	19
nobora	nai	nobotta	climb [a mountain]	19
noma	nai	nonda	drink	6
noma	nai	nonda	take [medicine]	17
nora	nai	notta	ride, get on [a train]	16
nuga	nai	nuida	take off (clothes, shoes, etc.)	17
oka	nai	oita	put	15
okura	nai	okutta	send	7
okura	nai	okutta	escort [someone], go with	24
omowa	nai	omotta	think	21
omoidasa	nai	omoidashita	remember, recollect	15
osa	nai	oshita	push, press	16
owara	nai	owatta	finish	4
oyoga	nai	oyoida	swim	13
sawara	nai	sawatta	touch [a door]	23

	masu-form	te-form	dictionary form
shirimasu	shiri masu	shitte	shiru
suimasu [tabako o ~]	sui masu	sutte	suu
sumimasu	sumi masu	sunde	sumu
suwarimasu	suwari masu	suwatte	suwaru
tachimasu	tachi masu	tatte	tatsu
tetsudaimasu	tetsudai masu	tetsudatte	tetsudau
tomarimasu [hoteru ni ~]	tomari masu	tomatte	tomaru
torimasu	tori masu	totte	toru
torimasu [shashin o ~]	tori masu	totte	toru
torimasu [toshi o ~]	tori masu	totte	toru
tsukaimasu	tsukai masu	tsukatte	tsukau
tsukimasu [eki ni ~]	tsuki masu	tsuite	tsuku
tsukurimasu	tsukuri masu	tsukutte	tsukuru
tsurete ikimasu	tsurete iki masu	tsurete itte	tsurete iku
ugokimasu [tokei ga ~]	ugoki masu	ugoite	ugoku
urimasu	uri masu	utte	uru
utaimasu	utai masu	utatte	utau
wakarimasu	wakari masu	wakatte	wakaru
watarimasu [hashi o ~]	watari masu	watatte	wataru
yaku ni tachimasu	yaku ni tachi masu	yaku ni tatte	yaku ni tatsu
yasumimasu	yasumi masu	yasunde	yasumu
yasumimasu [kaisha o ~]	yasumi masu	yasunde	yasumu
yobimasu	yobi masu	yonde	yobu
yomimasu	yomi masu	yonde	yomu

nai-form		ta-form	meaning	lesson
shira	nai	shitta	get to know	15
suwa	nai	sutta	smoke [a cigarette]	6
suma	nai	sunda	be going to live	15
suwara	nai	suwatta	sit down	15
tata	nai	tatta	stand up	15
tetsudawa	nai	tetsudatta	help (with a task)	14
tomara	nai	tomatta	stay [at a hotel]	19
tora	nai	totta	take, pass	14
tora	nai	totta	take [a photograph]	6
tora	nai	totta	grow old	25
tsukawa	nai	tsukatta	use	15
tsuka	nai	tsuita	arrive [at the station]	25
tsukura	nai	tsukutta	make, produce	15
tsurete ika	nai	tsurete itta	take (someone)	24
ugoka	nai	ugoita	[a watch] move, work	23
ura	nai	utta	sell	15
utawa	nai	utatta	sing	18
wakara	nai	wakatta	understand	9
watara	nai	watatta	cross [a bridge]	23
yaku ni tata	nai	yaku ni tatta	be useful	21
yasuma	nai	yasunda	take a rest, take a holiday	4
yasuma	nai	yasunda	take a day off [work]	11
yoba	nai	yonda	call	14
yoma	nai	yonda	read	6

II-group

	masu-form	te-form	dictionary form
abimasu [shawā o ~]	abi masu	abite	abiru
agemasu	age masu	agete	ageru
akemasu	ake masu	akete	akeru
atsumemasu	atsume masu	atsumete	atsumeru
dekakemasu	dekake masu	dekakete	dekakeru
dekimasu	deki masu	dekite	dekiru
demasu [kissaten o ~]	de masu	dete	deru
demasu [daigaku o ~]	de masu	dete	deru
demasu [otsuri ga ~]	de masu	dete	deru
hajimemasu	hajime masu	hajimete	hajimeru
imasu	i masu	ite	iru
imasu [kodomo ga ~]	i masu	ite	iru
imasu [Nihon ni ~]	i masu	ite	iru
iremasu	ire masu	irete	ireru
iremasu [kōhii o ~]	ire masu	irete	ireru
kaemasu	kae masu	kaete	kaeru
kaemasu	kae masu	kaete	kaeru
kakemasu [denwa o ~]	kake masu	kakete	kakeru
kakemasu [megane o ~]	kake masu	kakete	kakeru
kangaemasu	kangae masu	kangaete	kangaeru
karimasu	kari masu	karite	kariru
kimasu [shatsu o ~]	ki masu	kite	kiru
ki o tsukemasu [kuruma ni ~]	ki o tsuke masu	ki o tsukete	ki o tsukeru
kuremasu	kure masu	kurete	kureru
makemasu	make masu	makete	makeru
mimasu	mi masu	mite	miru
misemasu	mise masu	misete	miseru
mukaemasu	mukae masu	mukaete	mukaeru
nemasu	ne masu	nete	neru
norikaemasu	norikae masu	norikaete	norikaeru

nai-form		ta-form	meaning	lesson
abi	nai	abita	take [a shower]	16
age	nai	ageta	give	7
ake	nai	aketa	open	14
atsume	nai	atsumeta	collect, gather	18
dekake	nai	dekaketa	go out	17
deki	nai	dekita	be able to, can	18
de	nai	deta	go out [of a coffee shop]	13
de	nai	deta	graduate from [university]	16
de	nai	deta	[change] come out	23
hajime	nai	hajimeta	start, begin	14
i	nai	ita	exist, be (animate things)	10
i	nai	ita	have [a child]	11
i	nai	ita	stay, be [in Japan]	11
ire	nai	ireta	put in, insert	16
ire	nai	ireta	make [coffee]	24
kae	nai	kaeta	exchange, change	18
kae	nai	kaeta	change	23
kake	nai	kaketa	make [a telephone call]	7
kake	nai	kaketa	put on [glasses]	22
kangae	nai	kangaeta	think, consider	25
kari	nai	karita	borrow	7
ki	nai	kita	put on [shirt, etc.]	22
ki o tsuke	nai	ki o tsuketa	pay attention [to cars], take care	23
kure	nai	kureta	give (me)	24
make	nai	maketa	lose, be beaten	21
mi	nai	mita	see, look at, watch	6
mise	nai	miseta	show	14
mukae	nai	mukaeta	go to meet, welcome	13
ne	nai	neta	sleep, go to bed	4
norikae	nai	norikaeta	change (trains, etc.)	16

	masu-form		te-form	dictionary form
oboemasu	oboe	masu	oboete	oboeru
okimasu	oki	masu	okite	okiru
orimasu [densha o 〜]	ori	masu	orite	oriru
oshiemasu	oshie	masu	oshiete	oshieru
oshiemasu [jūsho o 〜]	oshie	masu	oshiete	oshieru
shimemasu	shime	masu	shimete	shimeru
shirabemasu	shirabe	masu	shirabete	shiraberu
sutemasu	sute	masu	sutete	suteru
tabemasu	tabe	masu	tabete	taberu
tarimasu	tari	masu	tarite	tariru
tomemasu	tome	masu	tomete	tomeru
tsukaremasu	tsukare	masu	tsukarete	tsukareru
tsukemasu	tsuke	masu	tsukete	tsukeru
umaremasu	umare	masu	umarete	umareru
wasuremasu	wasure	masu	wasurete	wasureru
yamemasu [kaisha o 〜]	yame	masu	yamete	yameru

nai-form		ta-form	meaning	lesson
oboe	nai	oboeta	memorize	17
oki	nai	okita	get up, wake up	4
ori	nai	orita	get off [a train]	16
oshie	nai	oshieta	teach	7
oshie	nai	oshieta	tell [an address]	14
shime	nai	shimeta	close, shut	14
shirabe	nai	shirabeta	check, investigate	20
sute	nai	suteta	throw away	18
tabe	nai	tabeta	eat	6
tari	nai	tarita	be enough, be sufficient	21
tome	nai	tometa	stop, park	14
tsukare	nai	tsukareta	get tired	13
tsuke	nai	tsuketa	turn on	14
umare	nai	umareta	be born	22
wasure	nai	wasureta	forget	17
yame	nai	yameta	quit or retire from [a company], give up	16

III−group

	masu-form		te-form	dictionary form
annai-shimasu	annai-shi	masu	annai-shite	annai-suru
benkyō-shimasu	benkyō-shi	masu	benkyō-shite	benkyō-suru
denwa-shimasu	denwa-shi	masu	denwa-shite	denwa-suru
hikkoshi-shimasu	hikkoshi-shi	masu	hikkoshi-shite	hikkoshi-suru
kaimono-shimasu	kaimono-shi	masu	kaimono-shite	kaimono-suru
kekkon-shimasu	kekkon-shi	masu	kekkon-shite	kekkon-suru
kengaku-shimasu	kengaku-shi	masu	kengaku-shite	kengaku-suru
kenkyū-shimasu	kenkyū-shi	masu	kenkyū-shite	kenkyū-suru
kimasu	ki	masu	kite	kuru
kopii-shimasu	kopii-shi	masu	kopii-shite	kopii-suru
motte kimasu	motte ki	masu	motte kite	motte kuru
renshū-shimasu	renshū-shi	masu	renshū-shite	renshū-suru
ryūgaku-shimasu	ryūgaku-shi	masu	ryūgaku-shite	ryūgaku-suru
sanpo-shimasu [kōen o ～]	sanpo-shi	masu	sanpo-shite	sanpo-suru
sentaku-shimasu	sentaku-shi	masu	sentaku-shite	sentaku-suru
setsumei-shimasu	setsumei-shi	masu	setsumei-shite	setsumei-suru
shimasu	shi	masu	shite	suru
shinpai-shimasu	shinpai-shi	masu	shinpai-shite	shinpai-suru
shōkai-shimasu	shōkai-shi	masu	shōkai-shite	shōkai-suru
shokuji-shimasu	shokuji-shi	masu	shokuji-shite	shokuji-suru
shūri-shimasu	shūri-shi	masu	shūri-shite	shūri-suru
shutchō-shimasu	shutchō-shi	masu	shutchō-shite	shutchō-suru
sōji-shimasu	sōji-shi	masu	sōji-shite	sōji-suru
tsurete kimasu	tsurete ki	masu	tsurete kite	tsurete kuru
unten-shimasu	unten-shi	masu	unten-shite	unten-suru
yoyaku-shimasu	yoyaku-shi	masu	yoyaku-shite	yoyaku-suru
zangyō-shimasu	zangyō-shi	masu	zangyō-shite	zangyō-suru

nai-form		ta-form	meaning	lesson
annai-shi	nai	annai-shita	show around, show the way	24
benkyō-shi	nai	benkyō-shita	study	4
denwa-shi	nai	denwa-shita	phone	20
hikkoshi-shi	nai	hikkoshi-shita	move (house)	23
kaimono-shi	nai	kaimono-shita	do shopping	13
kekkon-shi	nai	kekkon-shita	marry, get married	13
kengaku-shi	nai	kengaku-shita	visit some place for study	18
kenkyū-shi	nai	kenkyū-shita	do research	15
ko	nai	kita	come	5
kopii-shi	nai	kopii-shita	copy	14
motte ko	nai	motte kita	bring (something)	17
renshū-shi	nai	renshū-shita	practice	19
ryūgaku-shi	nai	ryūgaku-shita	study abroad	25
sanpo-shi	nai	sanpo-shita	take a walk [in a park]	13
sentaku-shi	nai	sentaku-shita	wash (clothes)	19
setsumei-shi	nai	setsumei-shita	explain	24
shi	nai	shita	do	6
shinpai-shi	nai	shinpai-shita	worry	17
shōkai-shi	nai	shōkai-shita	introduce	24
shokuji-shi	nai	shokuji-shita	have a meal, dine	13
shūri-shi	nai	shūri-shita	repair	20
shutchō-shi	nai	shutchō-shita	go on a business trip	17
sōji-shi	nai	sōji-shita	clean (a room)	19
tsurete ko	nai	tsurete kita	bring (someone)	24
unten-shi	nai	unten-shita	drive	18
yoyaku-shi	nai	yoyaku-shita	reserve, book	18
zangyō-shi	nai	zangyō-shita	work overtime	17

Contributors

田中よね　*Yone Tanaka*
The Association for Overseas Technical Scholarship
Matsushita Electric Industrial Co., LTD. Overseas Training Center
Coordinator of Japanese Language Course

牧野昭子　*Akiko Makino*
The Association for Overseas Technical Scholarship
The Japan Foundation Japanese-Language Institute, Kansai

重川明美　*Akemi Shigekawa*
The Association for Overseas Technical Scholarship
Matsushita Electric Industrial Co., LTD. Overseas Training Center

御子神慶子　*Keiko Mikogami*
The Association for Overseas Technical Scholarship
Matsushita Electric Industrial Co., LTD. Overseas Training Center

古賀千世子　*Chiseko Koga*
Kobe University International Students Center
Matsushita Electric Industrial Co., LTD. Overseas Training Center

石井千尋　*Chihiro Ishii*
YWCA Teachers' Association

Editorial Advisors

石沢弘子　*Hiroko Ishizawa*
The Association for Overseas Technical Scholarship

豊田宗周　*Munechika Toyoda*
The Association for Overseas Technical Scholarship

Illustrator

田辺澄美　*Kiyomi Tanabe*

写真提供
©オリオンプレス
栃木県
姫路市
広島県

みんなの日本語　初級Ⅰ
翻訳・文法解説　ローマ字版［英語］

2000年10月20日　初版第1刷発行
2004年6月24日　第5刷発行

編著者　株式会社　スリーエーネットワーク
発行者　髙井道博
発　行　株式会社　スリーエーネットワーク
　　　　〒101-0064　東京都千代田区猿楽町2-6-3（松栄ビル）
　　　　電話　営業　03(3292)5751
　　　　　　　編集　03(3292)6521
　　　　http://www.3anet.co.jp

印　刷　日本印刷株式会社

不許複製　　　　　　　　ISBN4-88319-165-6 C0081
落丁・乱丁本はお取替えいたします。

初級日本語教材の定番 みんなの日本語シリーズ

みんなの日本語初級 I

本冊	2,625円	漢字英語版	1,890円
本冊・ローマ字版	2,625円	漢字カードブック	630円
翻訳・文法解説ローマ字版（英語）	2,100円	初級で読めるトピック25	1,470円
翻訳・文法解説英語版	2,100円	書いて覚える文型練習帳	1,365円
翻訳・文法解説中国語版	2,100円	漢字練習帳	945円
翻訳・文法解説韓国語版	2,100円	聴解タスク25	2,100円
翻訳・文法解説スペイン語版	2,100円	教え方の手引き	2,940円
翻訳・文法解説フランス語版	2,100円	練習C・会話イラストシート	2,100円
翻訳・文法解説ポルトガル語版	2,100円	導入・練習イラスト集	2,310円
翻訳・文法解説タイ語版	2,100円	カセットテープ	6,300円
翻訳・文法解説インドネシア語版	2,100円	CD	5,250円
翻訳・文法解説ロシア語版	2,100円	携帯用絵教材	6,300円
翻訳・文法解説ドイツ語版	2,100円	B4サイズ絵教材	37,800円
標準問題集	945円	会話ビデオ	10,500円

みんなの日本語初級 II

本冊	2,625円	漢字英語版	1,890円
翻訳・文法解説英語版	2,100円	初級で読めるトピック25	1,470円
翻訳・文法解説中国語版	2,100円	書いて覚える文型練習帳	1,365円
翻訳・文法解説韓国語版	2,100円	教え方の手引き	2,940円
翻訳・文法解説スペイン語版	2,100円	練習C・会話イラストシート	2,100円
翻訳・文法解説フランス語版	2,100円	カセットテープ	6,300円
翻訳・文法解説ポルトガル語版	2,100円	CD	5,250円
翻訳・文法解説タイ語版	2,100円	携帯用絵教材	6,825円
翻訳・文法解説インドネシア語版	2,100円	B4サイズ絵教材	39,900円
翻訳・文法解説ロシア語版	2,100円	会話ビデオ	10,500円
翻訳・文法解説ドイツ語版	2,100円		
標準問題集	945円		

みんなの日本語初級　やさしい作文　1,260円

ホームページで新刊や日本語セミナーをご案内しております
http://www.3anet.co.jp

価格は税込です　スリーエーネットワーク

left lane Neeima / Niigata   6 oct -
                                 car in Re-polish
                                 4/11

        no 47
50 47   Ken-o Tsugarashima
        Do Not tak city exit. continue 2 km To JCT

Get supply - Right.
16 - 2 up Pas 1 street Past McDonalds
       left onto Hwy 44.
    at T-section Right to Kan-etsu Keno.
    So Towards Niigata   app 19 km.

    Exit 15 minakam   131 km
    291 left 7. 291   from Base

    ¥3850
                    Tenjin daira (gondola)
                                    14 km
                        okutone ski
                                    10 km
Intersection See white bridge ahead.
3.1 km Go left. towards central min akan
Mt. Tonigawadake
    291 ↓ 61
2. left   after okutones
2.5 km from toll.   construction
        63 → takaragawa.

    10.3 km. left at stop lights
    (Just after okutone signs.)
        windy Road up ↑
        tunnel Hōdaigi